ZOOM BEGINNER'S GUIDE 2021

Webinar Videos Are the Future in Teaching and Business. Master Zoom Meetings and Boost Your Business and Education.

ERIC SMITH

Table of Contents

Introduction 1
Chapter 1: Introduction Zoom 19
Chapter 2: Zoom Practice (Beginner's Guide) 70
Chapter 3: Zoom Practice (Advanced) 101
Chapter 4: Zoom For Work 138
Conclusion 145

INTRODUCTION

The massive use of smart working in this period is increasing the business of technology companies that offer tools for video conferencing, chat, and other applications that allow teams to stay connected virtually.

This book is a simple guide that seeks to equip you with the basic knowledge required to maximize the full potential of Zoom. The main idea of using Zoom is to connect and support people from a distance.

Zoom Meetings are the base of Zoom, and the term applies to video conference/meetings that use the platform to enable remote and co-located meeting attendants to interact frictionless. Since you don't need a Zoom account to attend a Zoom meeting, you can also remotely meet clients or hold interviews with remote candidates.

The Increasing Importance of Technology and Video Conferencing

Video conferencing is a visual form of conferencing which enables two or more persons to connect, relate, and interact with one another. This has, in no small measure, enabled smooth communication in organizations and businesses without necessarily having to move to one particular location. It is, however, becoming more popular by the day because of its ease of use and other benefits users stand to enjoy.

Video conferencing ensures you have a smooth and quality experience that is enabled through its integrated software. The software gives room for a number of activities through its encompassing features which enable you to schedule meetings, chat, email, screen share, vote amongst a host of other tools that enable institutions and organizations to hold productive meetings and receive instant inputs from attendees. Thus, the real-time effect of video conferences cannot be over-emphasized.

- *Enhanced Communication.* Video conferencing has enhanced communication among businesses and their employees, who are in different locations or time zones. Important events, schedules, and meetings can be seamlessly conducted with a large team over a video call. The integrated chat option with the service also enhances communication.

- *Manage Expenses and Time.* Business travel can cost a lot of time, money, and resources, both for the company and the employee. A simple switch to a video conference is potent in negotiating deals and saving money on fuel, expensive lunches, or traveling to another city for short meetings.

- *Enhanced Productivity.* With video calls, most of the participants are compelled to stay focused and get straight to the point. Participants are in sync with each other and it promotes brevity and straightforwardness. This is extremely pragmatic for completing projects faster. Also, with video conference meetings, we are assuming that you are working from home. This gives you more time, attention, and a comfortable environment to work more efficiently.

- *It helps to reach out to several people at the same time.* Video conferencing enables you to communicate and hold meetings with people from all over the world from the comfort of your home. In businesses, through video conferencing, ideas are raised by individuals, analyzed and finalized through the timely contributions of individuals who contribute visually. Also, presentations are done, and projects are completed faster and deals are concluded in no time.

- *It saves time and money.* Video conferencing saves the time that could have been used in traveling and saves the money that could have been used in transporting from one place to another, which is of great benefit for businesses as they get more returns. Hence, it plays a vital role in the reduced cost of keeping a business going.

- *It increases productivity.* With the attentiveness of all team members, who stay alert on the topic of discussion because they are being seen, video conferencing increases productivity due to managerial tools at hand.

- *It aids telecommunication.* Video conferencing is a step ahead of your normal audio calls. With flexible work timing, video conferencing could be a great way to fill the communication gap.

Better management is ensured when workers scattered in different locations are brought together, with their whereabouts and activities checked visually. Improved teamwork and capabilities and better results are gotten from group projects.

From the foregoing, video conferencing is beneficial for businesses, corporations, and institutions because it bridges the communication gap and allows for close monitoring and checks.

Video conferencing has ruled the corporate world for a decade, and its application is skyrocketing constantly. The impact of this technology has become so widespread that 36% of US white-collar professionals prefer a video conferencing capability in the workplace, or at home, over a pay raise.

FREELANCERS AND DIGITAL NOMADS

Freelancing is no longer a destitution when it comes to earning a steady income and having a stable job. In fact, it is the new euphemism for a progressive and exciting career that offers new opportunities with each passing day. Not only can you work from the comfort of your own home, but you also have the freedom of choosing your own schedule and taking days off as you please. A major part of this flexibility and prerogative can be attributed to the rise of technology and the invention of conducive digital tools.

Freelancers and digital nomads (people who work remotely to access the benefits of flexibility and time management) have risen in number over the past five years due to the advancement in technology and digital tools, such as video conferencing services, project management software, and other necessary tools specific to particular domains (cloud communications and productivity tools). This has also led multiple companies to embrace the concept of hiring more and more freelancers and digital nomads. In the beginning, people were in constant fear of running out of money or ending up nowhere, which led to only the 'adventurous' professionals to seek freelancing. But since numerous companies are supporting this apprehension, experts of all fields are quitting their full-time office jobs and becoming digital nomads to work from the comfort of their homes.

Since the advent of video conferencing, most freelancers, and even businessmen, have been utilizing this pragmatic tool that offers numerous benefits. Firstly, these services bolster the thought of most professionals - "a meeting that could have been an email."

Video conferencing not only helps to reduce your commute time but also saves part of your paycheck.

Since these services are taking a new dimension, freelancers and digital nomads are able to communicate effectively with their clients all around the world. In fact, freelancers should use this prevailing tool more often to conduct virtual meetings with their clients on a regular basis. This not only portrays your seriousness regarding your work but also provides assurance or proof of getting work done, along with proof of who you are.

Here are a few other prominent reasons why you should make use of this favorable service more often as a freelancer:

- *Elevate your Brand Identity.* With regular video conference calls, you get an opportunity to formally greet your clients every now and then. Connecting with your clients virtually can build a trusting bond through a subtle display of expression and knowing each other face-to-face. This approach is more than just a face for your brand. It adds personality and substance to your brand image.

- *Learn More.* Emails and forwarded documents are usually concise and to-the-point. While these are typically useful in keeping deadlines and details straightforward, you can also learn a thing or two about a project on a video call. This provides additional details that can revamp the assignment entirely.

- *Share Results.* Quite often, the results or reports you share through emails are indecipherable. The person receiving them might consider them redundant due to difficulties in understanding. This is when video conferencing can be used to your advantage. You can personalize your video calls and explain complicated data to your clients through features like screen sharing and real-time chat operations. As soon as your clients are offered a better understanding and are made aware of the highlights of the results or reports, they can see the work for what it is and continue their future agreements with you.

Video conferencing is an absolute boon for freelancers and digital nomads. These virtual wage earners can effortlessly hold virtual meetings and schedule face-to-face appointments. It is specifically favorable for those who reside on the other side of the globe. Let's not forget the huge amount of money that can be saved by avoiding insignificant cross-city and cross-country trips.

SOCIAL DISTANCE: THE NEW CHALLENGE

Currently, the world is facing a mortifying pandemic and most people are advised to stay at home to prevent COVID-19 from spreading further. This horrific situation has not only ruined normal business operations but has also impacted our social lives. Large-scale conferences and events, such as Milan Design Week, Google's annual developer's conference, tech and music festival SXSW, major sports events like Formula 1, and even the Olympics have been canceled this year to avoid public gatherings and respect the norms of social distancing.

In this situation, people are trying to conduct business, conferences, and necessary meetings through video calls. A few months ago, video conferencing services were mere conveniences or added benefits to any work environment but with the obligation of social distancing, these have quickly become a necessity. Employees have to work from home, and video calls are one of the ways to stay connected with your boss, colleagues, clients, or students if you are a teacher. Students are duty-bound to learn online, though lessens that are conducted over video conferences. Because of this, teachers, businessmen, lawyers, and most employees in general, are trying to learn this new technology.

Enter Zoom. This name was barely known across the world before COVID-19 struck and pushed people to stay at home. Almost every business, school, university, and the informal party started using Zoom, which led to a massive surge in its popularity, so much so, that the company noted 2.2 million new users every month over the past few months (since the lockdown measures were established). Its overnight success made it a popular name in every household. It's almost a given that you have heard the name a few times during this lockdown.

If you aren't entirely familiar with it, let us break it down for you. Zoom is a video conferencing platform that allows multiple users to access relevant video conference meetings at the same time. Whether it is your office meeting or a virtual gathering with your long-distance family, Zoom can keep you connected at all times.

In the past, Zoom was only aimed at big corporations, businesses with large teams, or companies that worked with virtual assistants or digital nomads. With the recent practice of social distancing, most of the companies and clients are switching to Zoom to stay connected and keep the work flowing. While companies that require a physical presence have suffered tremendously, video conferences have greatly aided the companies that are able to work virtually.

The following chapters will provide a detailed description of Zoom and teach you how to begin using this handy tool today.

Some Benefits of Working from Home

The world is growing rapidly; so is the approach in the workforce and all there is to businesses and organizations. In the past few years, working from home (also known as remote working) has been gaining prominence amongst the workforce. This approach has, however, aided the advancement of telecommunication because of the necessity to communicate with a wide range of people at different locations. Without mincing words, some of the benefits of working from home include:

- Flexibility: It is left to your prerogative to take breaks at any time, take a nap or unwind. The most important part is to get your work done and meet target deadlines.
- Concentration: You are at a greater advantage of paying attention to the work at hand rather than battling with distractions from co-workers or the events at the office.
- Finance: You wouldn't have to spend on transport or getting corporate dresses when you

work from the comfort of your home. Thus, you easily save up and invest.

- Convenience: When you work remotely, there wouldn't be a reason to get stuck in early morning rush, traffic, or other unforeseen delaying occurrences.
- Significant others: You have more time to make calls and attend to family and loved ones since you don't work under any stringent schedule or timing. You tend to be happier.
- Productivity: A Stanford study has revealed that employees who work remotely are 13 percent more effective than their counterparts who work in the office.
- Affordability: As an employer of labor or an entrepreneur, allowing your workers to work from home is cheaper and more affordable compared to the expenses attached to getting an office space, refurbishing it to your taste, getting the essential office equipment, and drawing salary structure that would cover the employees' expenses throughout the month.

- Competence: Working from home simply implies the openness and ability to work with anyone in the world.
- Diversity: When employees are employed from dispersed areas from around the world, they bring to the table great and diversified ideas based on their different experiences, which would in no small measure create an insight into the local and international market.
- Increased loyalty: Because of the convenience attainable in working remotely, employees tend to be happier and loyal.
- Consistency: Working from home gives room for freedom of employees. Thus, they won't constantly see the need for vacations.
- Surprisingly, employees will be more committed and thus work longer on a day-to-day basis as the need arises.

VIRTUAL MEETING ETIQUETTES

As much as virtual meetings are encouraged due to their earlier discussed benefits, there are rules or etiquettes every professional should know. To help keep your meetings professional and productive, follow these virtual meeting etiquette tips and rules.

- Dress well. In truth, working remotely gives room for freedom to put on anything to work. No matter how tempted you might get or how lazy you might feel, take a few minutes to put on clean, presentable clothes and groom your hair.
- Be conscious of your surroundings. You might get overwhelmed or overly excited talking with your co-workers. Yet, adjust your work setup to give room for enough lighting, and ensure your background is work-appropriate and professional. This means no beds in the background, no dirty or rough rooms, and no noise from kids or barking of dogs.
- Mute your microphone when you are not talking. Ensure you join the meeting with your microphone on mute, and mute the microphone when you are not speaking. This gives other participants the ability to share their thoughts without distractions.

- Speak up. Ensure you announce yourself when you join a small meeting of around two to five persons. You can do this by saying a simple "Hello" so as to ensure you don't interrupt someone mid-sentence.
- Always project your voice.
- Do away with food. Eating snacks distracts you from the focus of the meeting and also distracts other participants. Instead of concentrating on the task being discussed, you tend to worry about dropping crumbs over your keyboard.
- Sit up and be attentive. Don't be tempted to check your inbox or carry on a side conversation when a meeting is going on. Aside from the fact that you might miss out on important information, you might also miss the chance to share your views and ideas. Also, don't let your eyes wander around too much, and don't make big extraneous movements.
- Avoid pressing the keyboard. When a virtual meeting is on, avoid pressing your keyboard. The sound of your typing is distracting, and prevents you from concentrating fully. For

optimal concentration, get a quality headset or pick up your notepad and pen to take meeting notes.

CHAPTER 1:
INTRODUCTION ZOOM

What Is Zoom?

Zoom is a cloud-oriented video conference service where a person meets others either by video or just by voice, or both. All this happens via a live conversation. Zoom lets you record these sessions for later viewing as well. The software has gained global acceptance due to its sleek performance and availability.

Zoom was launched in 2011 but has recently garnered a lot of attention due to the coronavirus pandemic. Whether it is for online classes, business meetings, informal gatherings, or group practices, Zoom seems to be the preferred tool for staying connected to the outside world amidst this gloomy quarantine. And, with the numerous entertaining and unique features, it is highly preferred when compared to the other video conferencing services.

Since its launch, Zoom has not only been very popular in Europe and the United States but has also boomed all across the world. Unlike other video conferencing services that allow no more than 4-5 people to share a screen at one time, Zoom allows hundreds of participants at a time (based on your subscription plan).

But, with so many other video conferencing services available, what is the appeal of Zoom, and what has led people to use this platform more than other services? Apart from its riveting features, it all boils down to its reliability and accessibility.

A Zoom session refers to a video conference meeting held with Zoom. These meetings can be joined by webcam or phone. Similarly, the Zoom room is a physical hardware setting that allows companies to organize and start Zoom meetings from their conference rooms. The Zoom room requires an additional order to the Zoom plans and is the ideal solution for large companies.

KEY FEATURES OF ZOOM

Single meetings: Host unlimited meetings one by one, even with a free schedule.

Group meetings: Host up to 500 attendees (if you purchase the "big meeting" extension). A free program allows you to host up to 40 minutes of video conferencing with up to 100 participants.

Screen sharing: Meet individually or with large groups and share the screen with them so they can see what you see.

How to select Zoom plans

Zoom enables one-on-one discussion time that can grow into group calls, vocations, training workshops for internal and external audiences, and international video conferences with up to 1,000 participants and up to 49 screen videos. Freebies allow unlimited meetings one by one but limit group time to 40 minutes and 100 participants. The paid plan starts at $15 per month per host.

Zoom Plans:

Zoom Unpaid:

This level is free, and one can hold an unrestricted number of meetings. Multi-participant group meetings are up to 40 minutes long and cannot be recorded.

Zoom Pro (paid):

This level bears $14.99/£11.99 per month for meeting guests. It allows hosts to create personalized meeting credentials for recurring Zoom meetings and allows you to store meetings in the cloud or on your device. It includes a 24-hour group meeting.

Zoom Business:

This level bears $19.99/£15.99 per month for meeting guests (minimum 10). It allows you to tag Zoom meetings with trash URLs and company brands, and a copy of Zoom stored meetings along with a dedicated service center.

Zoom Enterprise:

This level costs $19.99/£15.99 per month and for event attendees (minimum 100) and is for businesses with more than 1,000 employees. It provides uncapped cloud storage, customer manager success, and discounts in webinars and Zoom rooms.

Zoom Room (paid):

If you want to set up a room, you can sign up for a free 30-day trial. After the trial, you will be charged an additional $49/$39 per month and a room subscription, while Zoom webinars will cost $40/£32 per months and hosts.

BENEFIT OF USING ZOOM

Setting up a Zoom meeting is as easy as clicking an invitation link to launch the app or ask users to install the user interface.

No mass deployment solutions are required, and the user interface is easy and straightforward on both mobile and desktop devices.

Zoom also offers super-fast features with high-quality audio and video at any price.

Other advantages are discussed below:

Security

Although security was a controversial issue for Zoom, the company is committed to improving this factor. Zoom makes major changes to its security strategy and implements new features frequently. For example, all meetings now require host privileges and a password to participate.

Excellent support

Zoom offers fantastic user support for companies around the world. There is phone support in various time zones. You can quickly answer your questions whenever you need them.

Scheduling

You can also schedule meetings in advance using your Zoom app, which can connect to several other calendars, including those from Google and Microsoft. This makes it easier to connect everyone with the tools you love.

Another advantage of Zoom is that it constantly updates and improves what it can do with technology. With virtual backgrounds, you can eliminate the messy meeting room in the background of your call. There are also touch-up features for those who are concerned about their appearance.

Host controls in Zoom provide great control over how the meeting runs. You can create a co-host for your meetings by working with another consultant. There is also access to desktop sharing and transfer controls.

Zoom not only offers a seamless and futuristic experience but also makes it easy for your team to take care of things like virtual hand-raising. It also has other cool features.

Zoom vs Other Conferencing Tools

For remote teams, the most preferred collaboration software are Zoom, Skype, Facebook rooms, Google Hangouts, Microsoft Teams, ezTalks, Cisco Webex, and BlueJeans, etc.

All of these platforms can be used to hold video calls, chat, and host meetings or webinars. If you're looking for a new platform to help you do these things, you're probably considering platforms like these.

Ultimately, the variations between all of them may not seem significant. But the decision to implement one over another can still impact your team significantly. It's easy to say from the experiences of a remote team that every platform fits different needs, and that is why it is important to your decision to understand the pros and cons, features and pricing, etc. of these options.

Zoom vs Facebook Rooms

Since Facebook Messenger Rooms and Zoom are end-of-the-day video calling applications, we compared them both based on their functionality, availability, and more.

Facebook has finally revealed what its Zoom competitor, Messenger Quarters, can be renamed. The video calling application is integrated into the standalone Facebook Messenger app and is intended for personal use. In comparison, Zoom is based on technical video conferencing. But since both are end-of-day video calling apps, here is a comparison based on functionality, quality of the web, and more.

Availability

Both are present on iOS and Android when it comes to availability, and both have a web edition that can be obtained from anywhere. This means you can reach it on Windows OS, as well as on Mac and ChromeOS. What's more, you don't have to download a separate Messenger Rooms app, as it's built into the Messenger app itself.

Free or Not

One of the most significant benefits for the Facebook Messenger Room here is that it's free. Yes, you do not have to pay for any of the features as you do in Zoom. While Zoom also has a free tier, most of its features are restricted to the paid edition. Zoom has three paid plans costing $14.99 a month, and $19.99 a month. However, up to 100 participants are still in a benefit of the free version.

Characteristics

In this one, Zoom gets an edge as the video conferencing application can support up to 100 participants in one call session. The paid version can support from 350 to 500 participants. Comparatively, at the moment, Facebook Messenger Rooms are limited to 50 participants.

Yet when it comes to video call size, Messenger Rooms is taking the lead. It allows you to speak with 50 people for unlimited minutes at a time, whereas Zoom's free tier can support 100 (or less) participants in a 40-minute call. The paid version can support calls for up to 24 hours.

Since Zoom is designed for organizational use, it also has the function of call recording, something missing from Messenger Room right now. The biggest advantage of Facebook is the audience that it already has in the main app and the Messenger app. Using News Feed, Groups, and Events, you can start and share rooms on Facebook, and it's comfortable for people to drop by.

Facebook says it will quickly add ways to create Instagram Direct, WhatsApp, and Portal rooms. Both offer you the versatility to communicate text during a video call and share screens with others.

Skype vs Zoom

Several applications for video conferencing are on the market. Skype is among the competition's largest and oldest brands. It allows one-to-one video calls, instant messaging, screen sharing, group calls, and file sharing, much like Zoom.

Skype redirects messages to an email inbox for those who participate offline. Skype is still lagging behind its competition though, in that the platform only allows up to ten participants at a time. A no-go definitely for larger conferences.

According to Global Industry Forecasts, video conferencing is expected to become a 20-million-dollar industry by the end of 2024. With this growth, there are hundreds of platforms to choose from; "Zoom vs Skype" is just one of the companies' most popular debates.

Below is a comparison of Zoom and Skype features, pricing, and product performance to secure the best video conferencing needs.

Overview: Zoom vs Skype

Zoom

It's an innovative cloud-based with modern conference tools. Zoom provides breakout sessions that can be used to divide your viewers (e.g., customers or employees) into small groups for activities like webinar training and specific topical and online class discussions.

The organizer has the power to monitor the meeting to the fullest with Zoom. You can also mute all microphones when not in use, monitor presentation access for the attendants, and so on. Besides, this method allows the participants to participate by digitally raising their hands to the discussion.

The chat utility of Zoom also allows viewers to communicate directly with the instructor and other participants, thus ensuring a collective classroom setup.

Skype

Imagine communicating with your employees directly from your PC/phone through an instant short messaging service, screen sharing, file sharing, and informal/formal audio or video calls. Effective and direct—that's all about Skype.

Skype is designed to make simple communication using revolutionary technology. Its intuitive chat interface, like Zoom, allows users to send prompt messages to other users. Users can integrate video with audio from their chat windows without any effort.

General Information

When considering Skype vs Zoom, the biggest challenge is that they are both very powerful channels of communication. Deciding between these two can be difficult, as both are efficient and cost-effective.

By definition, Zoom provides software-based video and audio conferencing that was intended to promote collaboration through an advanced integrated system featuring web conferences, group messaging, and important online meetings.

On the opposite hand, Skype provides powerful tools for text, voice, and video, providing users with a smart way to share their experiences with others, no matter where they are.

Devices

Zoom supports web platforms such as Android and iOS.

Web-based Skype supports all Windows and Android devices, and iPhones.

Zoom has a variety of features, including video conferencing, streamlined scheduling, and collaboration between groups. This platform's other powerful features include local and cloud recording in premium audio feature, and in Zoom Meetings and Zoom Rooms.

Skype also comes with powerful chat tools, including Skype-to-Skype calls, community calls, call-forwards, one-to-one video calls, and instant messaging. You can send and exchange emails, video messages, displays, files, and contacts.

Designed for

Both Zoom and Skype are perfect for small and large businesses, but Skype's free plan is also popular with freelancers.

Pricing

Zoom offers four pricing packages for enterprises: Zoom Basic Plan, Zoom Pro Plan, Zoom Business Plan, and Zoom Enterprise Plan.

Basic Plan

The basic package, which is explicitly tailored for personal meetings, is free, can host up to 100 people, and provides one-on-one sessions without restrictions. It's an excellent gratuitous bid. You will use this program to:

- Meet for up to forty minutes
- Have a plethora of meetings
- Get the support online
- Enjoy the functions of web and video conferencing
- Make sure community collaboration is safe

Zoom Pro Plan

It is for the small teams, and it costs $14.99 per user per month. It comes with all the basic plan functionality and can accommodate 100 participants. You'll get unlimited meeting duration, assigned custom personal meeting ID, assigned scheduler, and reporting meetings.

This program also includes business interoperability, user management tools, admin controls, REST API, and Skype. Users can store and share large amounts of data with 1 GB data of MP4 and M4A cloud recording.

Optional Zoom Add-On Plans

They include five sub-plans:

- $40 per month for extra cloud recording storage.
- $49 per month for 323/SIP Room Connector.
- $49 per month for joining Zoom Rooms.
- $100 per month for toll-free dialing/Call Me.
- $40 per month for adding video webinars.

Business Plan

The business strategy for Zoom, which is worth $19.99 a month per user, is limited to smaller businesses.

Equipped with all of the Pro plan's functionality, mid-sized companies will use it to take their connectivity to another level.

The plan lets you host up to 10 hosts. It has an admin control dashboard, telephone support, and a vanity URL. The business plan is an excellent option if you prefer on-premise placement. Certain characteristics of the scheme include:

- Manage domains and one-way sign-on
- Client branding and customized emails
- Integration with LTI

Zoom Plan for Enterprise

Zoom Enterprise is for $19.99 per person/host per month. This plan includes all of the Business Plan features which need you to have a minimum of 100 hosts. Up to 200 participants are allowed on this plan.

The Enterprise package is ideal for large organizations with diverse meeting needs, with unrestricted cloud storage, a zealous client service manager, and executive company feedback.

Skype

Skype is free of charge. However, if you're looking to improve efficiency and increase revenue, Skype has a $2-per-month enterprise price package per user.

Business Plan

For Skype's Business Plan, users can use solid authentication as well as encryption to enjoy features like online meetings (250 participants) and secure communication lines.

Online Plan 2

This plan costs $5.50 a month per user and is designed for online business meetings. On Online Plan 2, you get:

- To join any equipment
- Enjoy HD video in the group as well as audio calling (for 250 people)
- Receive mobile technical assistance at the client level
- Office versions are available online
- 50 GB postbox

- 1 TB storage

Office 365 Professional Premium

This plan is for $12.50 per user per month. The Office 365 Company Critical plan has notable features, including:

- Government software pre-installed on PC / Mac
- Tablet and mobile apps

In addition, Microsoft's parent company Skype has supported Microsoft Teams over Skype as a forum for meeting and video conferencing. As a result, Skype support may diminish in favor of Teams over time.

Backend Integrations Zoom

Zoom supports:

- Microsoft One Drive
- Salesforce Box
- Slack
- Okta
- Microsoft Outlook
- LTI (Canvas, Desire2Learn, Backboard, and Moodle)

- Google Chrome
- Marketo
- Facebook Centrify
- Intel Unite
- Kubi
- Zapier
- RSA

Other integrations that Zoom supports include:

- Google Drive, DropBox, Pardot
- Firefox and Acuity Calendar
- Eloqua and the Microsoft Active Directory
- Hipchat, Infusionsoft, and HubSpot
- Skype
- Provides integration with such programs as:
- Office (Word, Lync, Outlook, PowerPoint)
- WordPress
- Mendix
- Lucid Meetings
- OnePage CRM
- Bitium
- Cayzu Helpdesk
- BigContacts

- SalesExec
- Interactive Intelligence CaaaS
- 1CRM
- Grasshopper
- Slack
- GroupWise

Skype can also be integrated with other systems, such as:

- CRM Agile
- Wimi and 88 Center for Virtual Touch
- Microsoft Dynamics Online CRM
- The Concierge and Yugma Moxie

Zoom vs Skype: The Low Line

Zoom and Skype both deliver customized solutions and are designed to take interactions from your company to the next level. However, the free and paid third-party enhancements apps enhance Zoom and give it a slight edge.

Zoom vs Google Hangouts

In 2013, Google Hangouts was released as a way to merge previously separate apps from the company, such as Google Talk (for calls), Google+ Messenger (for chat), and the original Google+ Hangout (for video) into one. Over time, the platform has added voice and video calling to accommodate all types of virtual conversations.

Zoom was released the same year in 2017. According to *The Business Journals*, it started climbing up the app charts. It has since gained traction, especially during the recent pandemic, when many people turn to the app for their (professional or personal) video conferencing needs, according to CNBC. Reuters reports that since January, the app has increased its daily active user base by 67 percent.

Number of Participants

The number of people a video conference app allows you to have in one meeting could be a make-or-break point for you, depending on whether you want to have a huge company-wide meetings (or are just super-popular).

Google Hangouts allows up to 160 people to chat but limits its video calls to only 25 persons per call (with the 10 most active participants shown at the bottom of the screen). This works for those who have meetings in small groups or just want to chat with some friends.

By contrast, Zoom allows users to have a video call with up to 100 participants. The **Gallery View** feature lets you see on one screen up to 49 of those participants. Plus, if you want an even bigger meeting, you can have up to 500 people (as long as you get the $50-month Large Meeting add-on).

Price

If you're only searching for a video conferencing device for friends and personal use, you may want to invest as close to nothing as you can.

If you only want to use Google Hangouts to make and receive phone and video calls, you can do this at no charge. But, if you wish for storage to keep records of your meetings and calls, pricing for 30 GB of storage starts at $6 per month.

Zoom has various packages, priced depending on how many features are included. The free choice allows you to have your meetings unlimited and up to 100 people. You pay $14.99 a month for a pro account (meaning for small teams) per host.

Additional Characteristics

Not everybody is using video conferencing software for video calls only. Often, it's good to learn that your apps can do more.

If you're searching for something a little easier, then your best bet is Google Hangouts. The software does have additional features, but most do not require extra practice. These include group conferencing, intelligent changeover, and integration with other Google apps. Most of the time, you can only log into and start using Google Hangouts.

At first, Zoom may seem a little more complicated, but it provides a great set of additional features if you'd like some fun. They provide a note-taking annotation tool, an automated transcript-creator, and even a touch-up feature.

Capabilities of Screen Sharing

Whether you're in a coworker meeting or talking to friends about that strange thing your cat did when no one was looking, you sometimes need visual aids. And if you're already on a video call, this is where the applications for screen sharing come in. Google Hangouts allows you to share your computer in the video call with others, but it is bounded to one user at a time.

By contrast, Zoom allows multiple people to share their screens at once within meetings.

GIFs & Emojis

This may not be the most prominent feature you're looking for, but sometimes your messages just need a little more fun. While this feature is more for those who talk with friends, you never know when you want to give a cool "thumbs up" emoji to your boss.

Google Hangouts lets you search and use a wide range of emojis (animated as well as unanimous) and GIFs. You can throw them into chats whenever you wish.

Although Zoom does not let you use emojis, it does allow you to use GIFs. Plus, it will enable admins to turn on and off the skill. This could be useful during meetings which should be all-business. But even so, you can still use the whiteboard capabilities of Zoom to draw on various slides and screens, so there is a way to get around that.

Time Limit

Google Hangouts has no known limitations regarding the length of calls you can make to others. Nevertheless, Zoom has a limit for those using its free package. And although you can make infinite numbers of calls, each call will last only up to 40 minutes. If you use a Pro account, or anything more expensive than that, the limit will move up to 24 hours.

Aside from learning about the features of an app, often it just takes you to use it and compare it to others firsthand to find out which choice is better for you. Happy chatting anyway!

Microsoft Teams vs Zoom

Which is better with Microsoft Teams vs Zoom? As the UC market is moving gradually from UC to UCaaS, the main competitive scenario that most customers are debating with us is no longer Skype for Business vs Cisco, but the cloud scenario (which now involves both video conferencing and audio, with a start (Zoom Phone functionality) of Zoom vs Microsoft Teams in the cloud. When it comes to comparing Microsoft Teams vs Zoom, the solution is just as tricky in the modern UCaaS environment now as it was in the old battle between Microsoft and Cisco.

Over the last couple of years, each of these relatively new platforms has seen rapid development, accumulating an impressive number of features and fans. Don't blink; the ongoing competition, creation and fulfillment of new scenarios for end-users and enterprises are likely to be rapid-fire over at least the next few years.

Many companies are currently in the Skype for Business mix. Still, with the recent announcement of the end-of-life date for Skype for Business Online (and speculation that the on-prem edition would have a similar fate), it is prompting many IT teams to resolve what their next step will be for their ecosystem of connectivity and cooperation.

So how do you decide between Zoom and Microsoft Teams? First, look at the breakdown of each platform, and then dive in to equate them as close as we can to a level playing field.

Zoom

Zoom is a pioneer (and potentially the pack's highest profile since its April IPO) in the video communications industry, addressing digital communications at all endpoints through their cloud platform for video, audio conferencing, collaboration, chatting, and webinars.

What is Microsoft Teams like?

Microsoft Teams is the all-encompassing work stream collaboration with Microsoft plus a centralized communications platform – connecting meetings, calls, chats, and file sharing with the Office 365 application stack to bring everyone together in a shared workspace.

Breakdown: Microsoft Teams vs Zoom

Microsoft Teams and Zoom both converge and compete at a very high level by providing a range of video conferencing tools (including room systems) and UC telephony services. By drilling more in-depth into the more complex functionality, usability, pricing, and alignment is how you can determine trade-offs and make the right decisions as to which platform is the match for your needs.

Characteristics

Where apps are concerned, both Zoom and Teams allow online meetings, conversations, calls, screen sharing, and file sharing. Microsoft's collaboration of Teams and its Office 365 platform is the difference between the two. This makes it possible for Microsoft Teams to be a one-stop-shop for many organizations.

This also allows seamless collaboration, backups, and the search for files. But going some way to complement the incorporation of Microsoft's Office365, Zoom and Slack features a wide-ranging relationship and a collection of technological combinations.

Zoom, as an organization, is a much newer organization than Microsoft's behemoth. Yet, it leads to competing with its aggressive roadmap, and because it doesn't have to worry about managing (and eventually leaving) a set of legacy customers at the premises.

UX (Utility Interface)

In Microsoft Teams vs Zoom debate, the user interface and experience are genuinely where Zoom excels. Zoom users are all raving about its simple interface and the ability to get end-users up and running with limited to no training or IT support.

Microsoft Teams faces a bigger challenge as users need to get a grip on communication in various networks and teams, integrated file sharing, and the other Office

365 apps built into Teams. Although the full range of interactive work stream features built into Teams obviously enables it to give a wider field of use (and therefore a greater value) than Zoom, this specific scope is also, in certain respects, its Achilles heel as regards aboard.

Room Systems

When areas of the arena Zoom vs Teams continue to become highly commoditized, one field of unique distinction is the "space systems" that are built within an enterprise. A room layout can range from a basic configuration of the huddle room to a deluxe conference room for executives. Although both provide app control, touch upgrades, mobile companion interactions, and dual-screen room support, Zoom has the added advantage of counting people, and Teams has proximity detection. Another distinction between Zoom and Microsoft Teams is that Zoom certifies all integrators and hardware suppliers while only the hardware solutions are approved by Teams.

Pricing

Microsoft Teams and Zoom offer each a free version of the platform, offering more advanced features with paid plans.

Microsoft Teams Free version includes restricted chat and collaboration services for productivity, meetings, calls, and security. Two large pieces that are missing with the free version include administration tools or support from Microsoft.

The free version of Zoom includes meetings that can host up to 100 participants (with a group meeting limit of 40 minutes), unlimited 1:1 meetings, online support, video and web conferencing features, group collaboration features, and security.

Microsoft's Premium plan is marginally cheaper per user than the equivalent Pro plan for Zoom, but they are priced equally with their corporate plans.

UC Telephony

The ability to make calls at an enterprise level is crucial, especially for video, audio, conferencing, and messaging business communications. This type of feature has initially been a stronghold of Microsoft, as Zoom did not initially have a phone system product.

Zoom Debate

The biggest win for Microsoft Teams is its tight, baked-in integration with Office 365 applications. Still, beyond that, Microsoft Teams has more than 70 combinations that include ticket management options, polls, weather, news, etc.

Integrations, usually, in the case of Microsoft, are to put user data into its network. On the flip side, Zoom is often added to other platforms as an integration. One great example of this is how Slack and Zoom work collectively. In addition to the Slack combination, Zoom has more than 100 combinations, including an Office 365 integration.

Zoom and Teams

If you are considering both systems running simultaneously, you would need a common management framework that works for both. This is just what PowerSuite does!

In reality, on both Teams and Zoom, we are increasingly seeing large companies choosing to "standardize." Microsoft Teams is excellent for internal collaboration, whereas Zoom is often preferred for external work, with customers or with guest vendors. Since they communicate with one another, it is simple for users to build specific scenarios.

Multiple platforms in the new digital workforce are becoming ever more the current standard. A study found in a recent survey that 85 percent of users use multiple platforms for collaborative apps.

Zoom vs ezTalks

The ezTalks cloud meeting is another neck-to-neck rivalry with Zoom. It boasts infinite number of user sessions, high-definition audio, and video access. Both apps allow users to hold conferences that have as many as 100 users at a time. Screen sharing and recording meetings are some of this program's other features. ezTalk also has a whiteboard and co-annotation interactive tools that Zoom just doesn't do

Nowadays, more and more business owners can accept online meetings in their day-to-day business work because it overcomes geographical and time barriers, enabling people from various regions/countries to hold or attend a meeting without any constraint simultaneously. This advance is accessible thanks to some program that provides online meeting solutions. Remarkably, ezTalks and Zoom are the two best video conferencing applications for these features. But there is a highly contentious topic connected with one being the right aid to hold a conference.

What is ezTalks?

ezTalks, a versatile cloud-based HD video conferencing software that features a fresh-looking user interface, leads to successful and seamless online education, online training, online meetings, online webinars, and online presentations, anywhere. It was widely used in all sectors, such as, industry, government, education, training, healthcare, legal, etc. The developers also offer a server version, in addition to the standard free version of ezTalks, for any company or organization to deploy on their own network. Even if you don't have any prior knowledge of using any such tools, ezTalks with integrated hardware and software can make the entire process completely simple and awesome.

Comparison: ezTalks vs Zoom

Features:

The resource you select will help the team with the procedures, workflows, reports, and needs that matter. When it comes to this, its features & functionality are important to consider. Then, based on some prominent features, here is a comparison of ezTalks with Zoom.

ezTalks:

- Group/Private high-quality video & audio
- Taping & Playback
- All-in-one Huddle Room video conferencing equipment
- Used on universal system platforms like iOS and Android

- Lots of built-in add-ons
- Secure, and best sharing of screens
- Supported dial-in phone service
- Control room management system for high-class meetings
- Safety and encryption;

Zoom:

- Sharing of web displays, community networking, and appearance at the same time
- Integration of H.323 / SIP in-room system
- MPEG 4 Client recording and recording in the cloud
- Remarks and co-annotation
- Encryption of a secure Socket Layer (SSL)
- Broadcast to YouTube or Facebook
- Virtual backdrop
- Cloud recording and playback

Pros and Cons

Although both are outstanding software for video conferencing with common aspects, they still have their respective strengths and weakness.

ezTalks:

Pros

- Safe to use one the Web
- Safety (One Time Password)
- As extensive as room for meeting
- Private and group chat in real-time, informal discussion and sharing, useful recording, and playback.
- Seamless desktop and mobile meetings (Windows, Mac, iOS, devices based on Android)
- Must only link to the Internet

Cons

- No available API

Zoom:

Pros

- Fast to set up (approx. 3 sec from download to install)
- Unlimited tier (up to 100 delegates)
- Specific industry plans
- Personal meeting ID customized.

- Unlimited duration for meetings of all sizes

Cons

- Priced according to host
- Cloud recording is a complement to the Basic plan.
- Need video conference codec and (payable) Cloud Connector account to connect

Pricing

Zoom provides four types of pricing plans at a starting price of $14.99/per, including the Basic, Pro, Business, and Enterprise plans. ezTalks provides three kinds of pricing plans, namely Starter Unlimited, Professional, and Business Plans at a lower $12.99/per host starting price. Both Zoom and ezTalks offer free trial options with the chance to enjoy screen sharing and online meetings. It is worth mentioning that ezTalks can be reached by phone call-in, and 100 mins free trial of the Webinar is available.

User Suggestions

ezTalks users can appreciate the ability to speak in front of the TV easily without being bound to their earphones or setting up a camera. What's more, along with its program, different useful features can only be found depending on the Internet, which is simple to manage. Even ezTalks allows each user to hold a meeting either as a group or as a private meeting. There are diverse choices to make. Yet Zoom's download is small, less than 10 MB in size, earning great customer reviews. Zoom provides the incorporation of more third parties than ezTalks. It's easy to use, but if you choose to add more participants, compared to other programs, it's a little costly.

Performance

These are excellent servers for the simultaneous sharing of documents, images, and videos from anywhere on your computer at any time. Although you cannot be present in person for any situation, you can use stereo audio and 1080p HD video resolution view operation to activate the application online. You may launch a one-click meeting with a specific meeting ID and invite the participants. You can enjoy smooth meeting controls with the help of these two items, such as the ability to mute or dismiss participants, and to "whiteboard" or annotate while sharing the screens. So, if you want to add more people or to increase the time limit, Zoom will cost more than ezTalks. You can test them with the free trials and compare their performance, respectively.

Bottomline

Online meetings are accessible and time-saving, and physical sessions are very interactive. Most of the best video conferencing applications can provide you with an efficient web conference experience that can save time and money. But which solution is stronger, and which is the app for top screen sharing? Computer ezTalks, or Zoom? In fact, the question isn't "which one is better?" but rather, "what program is right for your budget and needs?" Better software can undoubtedly boost employee productivity, teamwork, and save resources. Therefore, investing in a proper communication platform with a wide variety of features is essential for companies. ezTalks will do anything you want, with great convenience and a lower price for its superior services!

BlueJeans vs Zoom

Unlike Zoom, BlueJeans also specializes in the video conferencing environment, providing resources such as online video meetings, huddle rooms, and support for events. BlueJeans also offers features for social broadcasting, which enable users to publish content to social media. BlueJeans is a pioneer in its industry, offering consumers from all backgrounds a diverse variety of services and packages.

Meeting Room Products

At transforming the meeting room area, both Zoom and BlueJeans seem to excel. If you are looking for a small huddle-room solution or something more significant, you will find with any of these vendors the immersive video and audio conferencing services that you need.

Meetings of BlueJeans:

BlueJeans Meetings is an easy, convenient way for companies to access business-grade video calls with Dolby Audio High-Definition support. Users on any mobile device, conference room network, or laptop will immediately communicate with customers and coworkers. BlueJeans Meetings also offers services such as:

One-Click Scheduling: You can add a video call to any Outlook or Google Calendar with one button, without entering any code, passwords, or conference IDs.

Screen sharing and collaboration: Immediately share your new documents and video clicks or share the entire screen.

Dolby Voice Audio: High quality, high-definition sound with automatic suppression of background noise.

Easy Integrations: Improve efficiency with a range of Skype for company, workplace, and Slack integrations.

Cloud Sharing and Recording: Capture and exchange audio, video, and documentation meetings.

Verified security: Ensure a variety of secure deployment options.

Space compatibility: Users can access Polycom, Cisco, Life-size meetings, and a range of other space tech services based on the SIP.

Zoom Meetings:

Described as the leading company for video conferencing and online conferencing, Zoom has created an excellent meeting room solution for its clients. According to 2017 surveys, the company has a sector-leading net promoter score of 72. Zoom Meetings has the following features:

Online meeting services: HD audio and video support with screen sharing and collaboration for up to 500 video participants, app built-in.

Training services: Co-annotation and whiteboarding solutions, as well as a measure of attention to keep the participants focused.

Technical support: Facilities for quick start and enter, remote screen control, and more.

Integrated scheduling: Zoom operates with a built-in scheduling program for a client, including job addresses, mobile programming, and more.

Room Products

"Rooms" are evolving as a more common meeting room solution, as companies are searching for ways to integrate anything they need in a conference setting, including whiteboarding, networking, and video collaboration. Zoom and BlueJeans both provide their own exclusive room services.

BlueJeans Rooms

The BlueJeans Rooms service is designed to help companies transform any business space into a fully immersive video and audio conference room. BlueJeans Rooms allow people to be linked to any SIP conference room network and mobile or desktop users, including the following:

Wireless screen sharing functions: Display your laptop screen anywhere in the meeting room

Google and Microsoft Calendar Integration: Set up follow-up meetings to suit the schedule of all

Universal configuration features: The primary user interface comes with easy-to-read instructions and wrap-up reminders, so no training is required.

Central management: Customers can monitor any room in their BlueJeans network remotely, and identify problems with a live console.

Support services: Expand the size of an IT organization with a team of global conference experts from BlueJeans.

Zoom Rooms

Zoom provides a highly flexible and creative room experience based entirely on software, complete with optimized audio features, seamless camera systems, and wireless content sharing solutions. Such features of the Zoom Rooms include:

Integration with anyone: Via laptop, smartphone, and other conference system apps, everyone can access HD video and audio.

Wireless sharing: Dongles and cables are not required; you can easily wirelessly view content from a smartphone or laptop.

Starting with the one-touch meeting: Use voice commands and one-touch meetings to launch scheduled conferences or instant messaging on your calendar system.

Overview and management: From a single user interface to view and manage your conference rooms.

Native Integration: Zoom provides simple integration of microphones, tablet access, and all-in-one microphone output with a Crestron Mercury device.

Pricing

The program, delivered on a regular subscription basis by Zoom and BlueJeans, is close in several respects. After all, both organizations are committed to providing high-performance audio and video conferencing solutions to their customers within a diverse meeting room environment. Of course, one-way consumers can more quickly pick the service that's right for them is to look at the different prices and package packages.

Availability and Prices for BlueJeans

BlueJeans offers three separate kit and pricing options, including:

Me

Small business and person network, this program is available at £ 9.99 per host every month, allowing meetings of up to 50 members, connectivity from either computer or mobile device, and unlimited meetings. There is also access to Dolby Audio High Definition.

My Team

Built for mid-sized companies, this £13.32 kit allows up to 75 members to meet and includes cloud meeting recording, a dashboard command center, and historical meeting analytics. Users can also incorporate HipChat, Skype for Business, and Slack into My Team.

My Company

Optimized for the business world, My Company provides meetings for up to 100 attendees, along with support for room system schedule, personalized branding apps, and unrestricted cloud reporting. There is also a service for the control and monitoring of live meetings.

Zoom:

One area in which Zoom is different from its competitors is the packaging options. Zoom has a simple "free" version available to consumers, while many other companies do not offer the same option. Packages for the Zoom include:

- Basic
- Pro
- Business
- Enterprise

BlueJeans vs Zoom: What to choose?

Both Zoom and BlueJeans often get fantastic user feedback, offering a range of similar apps to choose from. Of course, both companies offer a free trial opportunity if you're looking to try something out for free before buying it.

No matter which contender you pick, you're sure to find that your enhanced conference program is improving your company communication and productivity.

CHAPTER 2:

ZOOM PRACTICE (BEGINNER'S GUIDE)

How to Download Zoom

The first step to correctly use Zoom is to download it from the official Download page. Depending on the operating system we use to visit the page, we will be presented with different download options. This is the download page that is displayed from Windows 10:

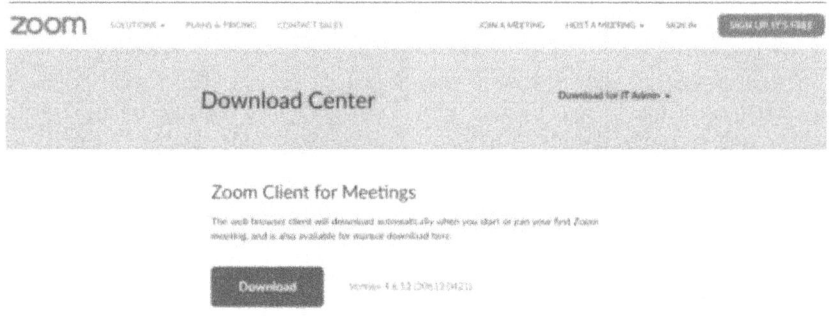

In the image below shows the page on an Android smartphone:

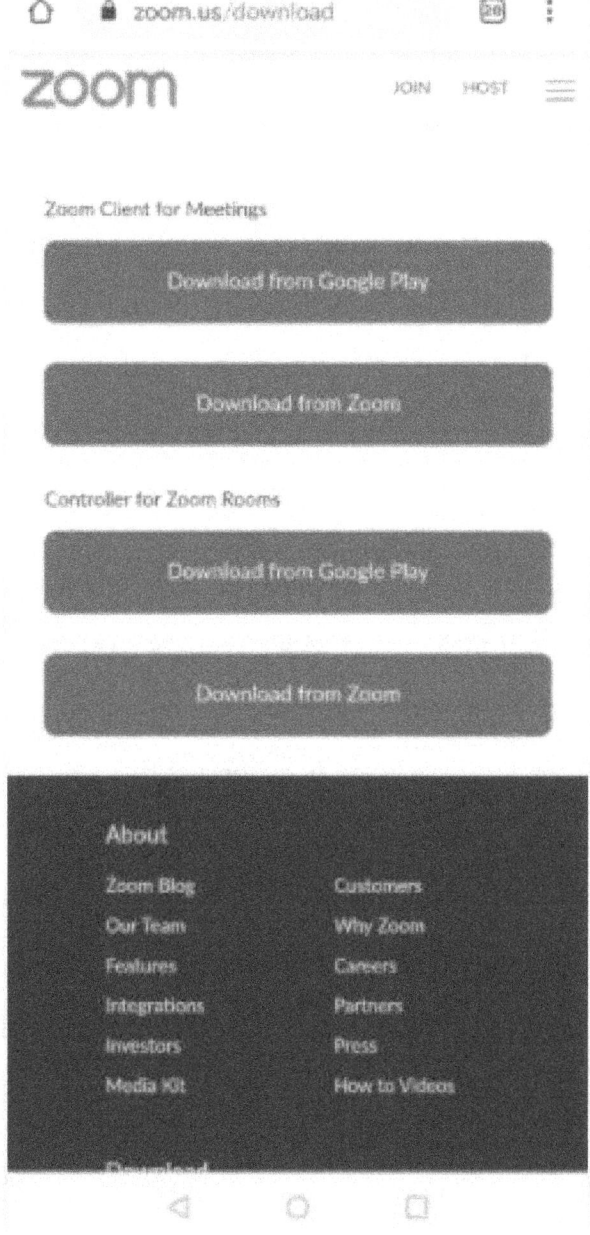

Downloading the Android app, unlike the iOS app (which is only allowed from Apple's App Store) is possible either from Google Play or as a manually installable APK.

How to Install Zoom

The installation of Zoom is very simple on all supported platforms. Let's first see the procedure to follow on Windows. Once you have downloaded the installer, *ZoomInstaller.exe*, you only need to double-click to start the installation.

We will be asked by Windows if we want the Zoom Meetings application to make changes to the device, we answer yes to continue. This will be the only choice to make, the procedure does not need other parameters to be successful. Once the installation is finished, we will be greeted by a screen with two buttons, **Join Meeting** and **Sign in**. The first one allows us to participate in a meeting; the other allows us to log in to the application in case we already have a registered account.

Install Zoom on Android

Even on Android, the installation procedure is very simple using Google Play. Just click on **Install** in Play Store and the app will be available on your smartphone. Slightly more complex is the installation procedure of the APK, the format on which Android applications are packaged. Installing the Zoom APK can be useful in case, for example, our Android smartphone does not have Google Play installed, a situation that many Huawei users are facing after the ban of Google apps on the Chinese manufacturer's phones.

The APK can be downloaded from your Android smartphone from the dedicated page. Just click on the file downloaded from the browser or use a file manager. The installation using a file manager is done by enabling the installation of unknown apps.

Install Zoom on MacOS

On Mac, the installation procedure is slightly more complex than on Windows because it involves changing some settings. You need to go to **System Preferences** (which can be called up by the Apple symbol in the top-left corner) and click on **Security and Privacy**. From here you have to click on the padlock symbol at the bottom left to enable the changes. Finally, select the option **App Store and developers identified** under **Allow apps downloaded from**. Once this is done, we can proceed to download Zoom from the official page. The file downloaded for macOS is *Zoom.pkg,* on which you just need a double-click to start the installation procedure, that in a few steps will allow us to have Zoom on our Mac.

Install Zoom on Linux

Zoom is also available for Linux in a version compatible with all the most popular distributions:

Ubuntu, Debian, Mint, CentOS, Red Hat, Fedora, OpenSuse, and Arch. If you don't use any of these distributions, you can download a compressed *tar.gz* package that contains the Zoom binary and all the necessary libraries.

On Ubuntu, the installation, allowed on version 14.04 and above, is extremely simple. You download the DEB for Linux from the download page of Zoom and install it with either a double click (which will open the graphical package management) or from the command line with *sudo dpkg -i Zoom*.deb*

CREATE A FREE ACCOUNT

On Zoom, you don't need an account to join a meeting, although if you are going to use it frequently it won't hurt to sign up. For hosting meetings, it is mandatory to create a meeting. In any case, the process is very fast, and you hardly need to give personal data.

You can register in Zoom on its website or from the application itself. In the app, tap on **Register** and enter your email address, name, and surname.

The email address must be valid since you must validate it through a message that will arrive in a few seconds. This email includes a link that you must visit to complete the registration and choose a password. Then, you have your account ready.

Create your First Meeting

One of Zoom's strong points is that it is very easy to use. One person - the host - creates the meeting and the rest can join by entering the meeting ID and password. You can create a new meeting from the **Meeting** chat screen by tapping **New meeting**.

New Meeting

With a standard version of Zoom, you hardly have any options to choose if you want to turn on the video or if you want to use your personal ID in the meeting. Tap on **Start the meeting** and in a few seconds, you will see yourself on the screen after you grant all the necessary permissions to the application.

Add Contacts

As we mentioned before, it is not strictly necessary that all the participants in a meeting make an account, although it will make your task much easier if the meetings are going to happen frequently. In such a case, it is a good idea to add people you frequently meet with as contacts.

To add a contact to Zoom, go to the Contacts tab. You can synchronize the phone contacts, although it is possible to search from the email address by tapping on the + button. Once you find the person you are looking for, press **Add** to send the friend request. The other person will receive the request and must accept it.

Join a Meeting

Creating a meeting is very easy with your application, and also joining one that is already in progress. If the host taps on the meeting identifier that appears superimposed on the screen (at the top), a link is generated that can be shared in messaging applications, so that other people can join directly.

It is also possible to do the exact same thing by writing the details by hand. On the main Zoom screen, you need to tap **Enter** and type in the meeting ID (a numeric code), and optionally what name you want to it to appear under. Before entering, you can choose if you want to connect without video and without audio.

Before the connection is fully made, you must enter the meeting password, which is useful to prevent uninvited people from joining. The password is visible by the host superimposed on the screen, just below the meeting identifier.

SETTING UP YOUR ZOOM ACCOUNT

Zoom has two different versions. One is free, and the other is the paid version. Although they have similar functionalities, there is a limit to the length of a meeting and the number of participants in the free version.

All you need to do to get an account is to go to *https://Zoom.us/* to get a free account. I will recommend you click on **Sign up with Google** or **Sign up with Facebook.**

It is more accessible to log in subsequently via Facebook or Google without having to worry about passwords.

10

You have free unlimited one-on-one meetings. However, when you have three or more people in your session, you are limited to forty minutes per meeting. After forty minutes, everyone gets kicked out. If you are expecting many participants in your meetings, I will recommend you upgrade to the paid version, so that you can get the unlimited length for your conferences and supports up to a hundred people.

Free Plan Offers:

- Unlimited one-to-one meetings
- Unlimited number of meetings
- Web conferencing features
- Online support
- Video conferencing features
- Security
- 40-minute limit on group meetings

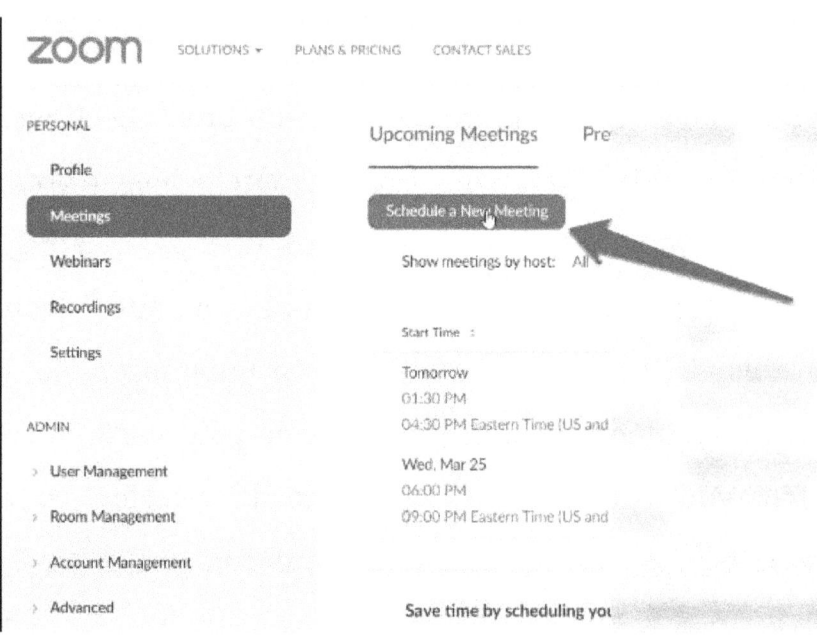

SHARE THINGS ON THE CALL

Zoom is more focused on work than other group calling alternatives like Houseparty, although you can do more than just call. The application has its own integrated messaging (in the Meeting and Chat tab), but during a call, you can also share all kinds of items.

Photos

To share photos from your gallery, with the possibility of making notes on it.

Document

To share documents as PDF files.

Box

To share files hosted in Box.

Dropbox

To share files hosted on Dropbox.

Google Drive

To share files hosted on Google Drive.

Microsoft OneDrive

To share files hosted on OneDrive.

Microsoft OneDrive for Business

To share files hosted in the business version of OneDrive.

Website Address

To share a webpage that opens and displays on the screen.

Share Whiteboard

Create a whiteboard and share it. Participants can also use it.

REACT AND RAISE YOUR HAND

Zoom supports meetings with up to 100 participants in its free version, so it can be difficult to clarify. For this, it has a digital version of something as basic as raising your hand to speak. Of course, it is not worth raising your hand for real, but you must use the **More** menu, then choose **Raise your hand**.

The host can see who has raised their hand, to decide whether to give you the floor or not. In addition to raising your hand, you can react to the presentation with the clap or like button, both available from the same menu.

Driving Mode

Meetings come when they come, and maybe it's your turn to meet at a time when you're busy. Zoom calls this mode Safe Driving Mode and is accessible by sliding the screen to the right. This mode turns your participation in the video conference into Push-To-Talk, or Walkie Talkie mode, i.e. with this mode activated, your camera is turned off and your microphone is muted, although with a touch of the push to talk button, the microphone will be activated until you touch it again. When you want to exit this mode you just need to slide to the left again.

Starting a Meeting

To start a Zoom meeting, open the Zoom app from your home screen or apps menu.

Click on **New Meeting**.

This starts the meeting immediately. You can use the drop-down menu below **New Meeting** for additional options.

You can choose to turn the video on or off.

This implies that you can host a meeting with or without video, this depends on you.

You can select if you want to make use of your Personal Meeting ID. (PMI)

This is a 10-digit number that is assigned to your account.

You can share your PMI with friends so they will be able to join any meeting you host using it.

If you don't enable the PMI option, your meeting will be given a random 10-digit number. use to invite other people to your meeting.

Clicking on **Start a Meeting**.

Clicking on **End Meeting**. Only do this when you are ready to end the meeting.

SCHEDULE A MEETING

To schedule a meeting:

Open the Zoom app.

Cancel	**Schedule Meeting**	Done
Date		4/28/20 >
From		3:00 PM >
To		3:30 PM >
Time Zone	GMT+1:00, West Africa Standard Time >	
Repeat		Never >
Use Personal Meeting ID (PMI) 581-417-2238		⚪

If this option is enabled, any meeting options that you change here will be applied to all meetings that use your personal meeting ID.

PASSWORD

| Meeting Password | | 🔵 |
| Password | | 9LrW3C |

MEETING OPTIONS

| Host Video On | | ⚪ |
| Participant Video On | | ⚪ |

Click on **Schedule Meeting**.

Set a date and time.

Set the duration i.e. how long the meeting would be.

Click **Time Zone** and select the time zone you want to use.

If you want the meeting to be repeated, i.e. if you want the meeting to be a recurring one.

You can also decide to choose if you want your video or off for you (the host) and the participants. Select **On** or **Off**.

OTHERS

To add an event

Select a calendar. This depends on the device you are using; you can add the Meeting to either Outlook Calendar, Google Calendar, or iCalendar.

You can also select advanced options. To do this, click **Advanced Options** and click the checkbox.

Advanced options include the following:

Enable Waiting Room:

This creates a virtual waiting room that attendees can wait in more like an actual reception room in companies. The host then decides who to allow into the meeting and when to admit each participant.

Enable Join Before Host:

This option allows participants to join a meeting before the host.

Mute participants on Entry (for PC and Mac only):

The host can decide to turn off the audio of participants.

Automatically Record Meeting:

This option automatically records the meeting and saves it for future viewing.

When you are done with all your settings preference, click **Schedule**.

Joining A Meeting

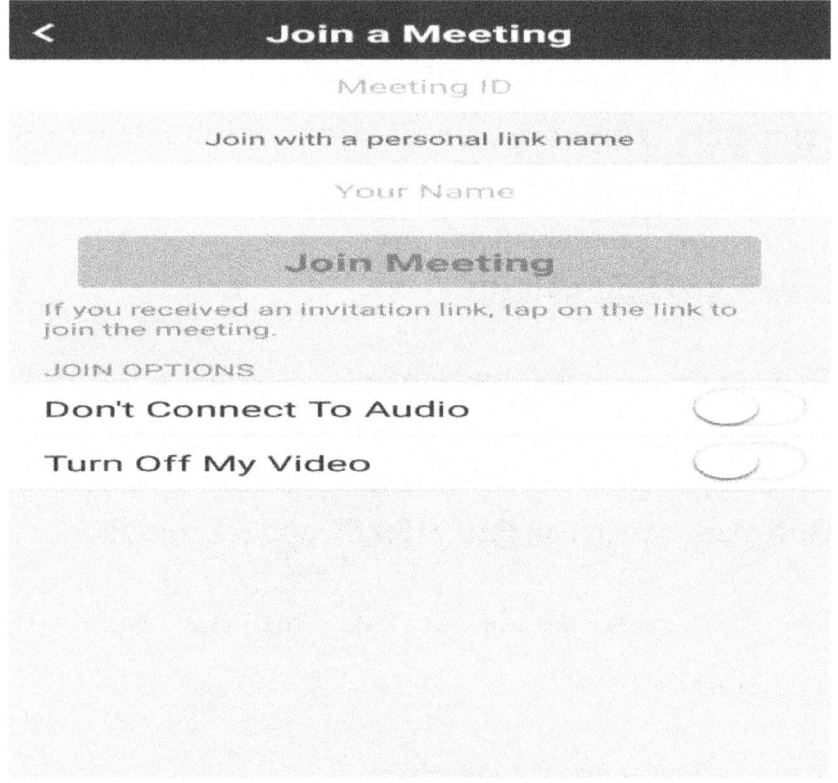

To join a meeting, you have to get the Meeting ID, a 10-digit number associated with each meeting.

If you are invited to a meeting by a host, you should receive a URL that ends with the 10-digit number of that meeting. Your invitation may be in the form of an email, instant message, or other means.

Click on the URL in the invitation to join the meeting via the Zoom app.

OPEN THE ZOOM APP.

Click or tap **Join Meeting**.

Input the Meeting ID **or the** URL.

You can turn off audio if you don't want the other participants to hear you, by clicking on **Don't connect to audio.**

You can turn off your video If you don't want the other participants to see you on camera during the meeting, by clicking on **Turn off my video.**

You can leave a meeting by clicking on **Leave Meeting.**

INVITING PARTICIPANTS TO A MEETING

To invite people to attend your Zoom meeting,

Open the Zoom app.

Connect to a meeting, either by starting a new meeting or joining an existing one.

To add participants, click on **Participants**. A drop-down menu then displays the names of all participants in the meeting.

Click on **Invite**, then select a messaging method, from here you can select a contact from your contacts list, or you can click on **Email** at top of the screen to send an already composed mail to your contacts. You can as well copy and paste the URL or invitation link in the email or choice of messaging.

Send your message by clicking on send. This automatically sends the message to your contacts.

AUDIO SETTINGS

First, you will tweak the audio settings. To begin with, find the **Join Audio** at the bottom-left corner of the window and click the arrow beside it. Click on **Audio Settings** from the dropdown menu.

A Settings window will pop up, which will look like this:

You can always access this window by clicking on the Setting icon on the top-right part of the screen.

• Once the window pops up, click on the dropdown list located on the right side of **Test Speaker** and select the speaker you prefer. You can either choose your headphone jack, your device's speaker, or any other speaker that is linked externally. We would recommend that you wear headphones as it will block out background noise, and keep your meeting private if other people are around.

• Next, you should check the microphone quality. Click on the dropdown menu on the right side of **Test Mic**. Depending on the microphone device you are using, select the relevant option. If you have an external microphone connected to your system, the list will display the name. If not, select **Same as system** to use the device's microphone.

- Then, you will check the input level of your microphone and voice quality. Start talking and view the slider beside **Input Level** as it transitions from red to green. Your audio is stable if you are in the green zone (not too slow and not too loud). Check the box beside **Automatically adjust microphone volume** to make it easier.

- Leave the other settings as they are. You can probably check the box that says **Join audio by computer when joining a meeting** to access the same setup as soon as you join a call.

VIDEO SETTINGS

Now, we will tweak the video settings. Click on **Video** located above **Audio** in the left panel.

The **Video Settings** box will look like this:

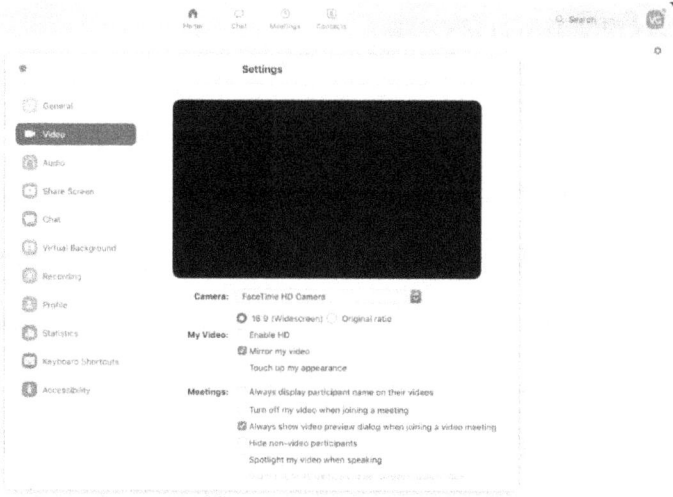

- As soon as you click on **Video**, a box appears with a message, 'Zoom would like to access the camera.' Click on **OK**. The black box in this picture will display what is seen by your front-facing camera. This is how the other participants will see you during the call. You can adjust your position and device to provide a clear view.

- If you have other devices or webcams attached externally to your video interface, select the device from the dropdown menu beside **Camera**. Leave the other settings as they are, and exit the box.

STOP VIDEO OPTION

Once your audio and video settings are in place, you are good to go. Close the setting page and click on the button **New Meeting** to start a meeting. If you need the call to be just audio, you can select the **Stop Video** option on the bottom-left corner of the window, as you access to the meeting.

SCREEN SHARING

To share your screen during a meeting, so others can see the contents of your screen:

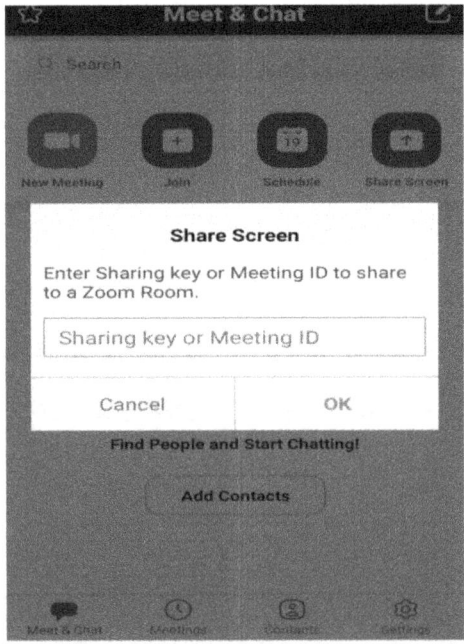

Open the Zoom app.

Connect to a meeting.

Tap the center of the screen (for mobile only).

Click on **Share Screen** or **Share Content.** It is located at the top of the screen on the iPhone and iPad. It is at the bottom of the screen on Android, PC, and Mac.

You can also click on the share screen before starting a meeting.

The next step is to select the app you want to share. You can also select **Whiteboard** which displays a white page suitable for drawing. You need to have a special plug-in on the iPhone and iPad to share your screen in a Zoom meeting.

ZOOM CALL RECORDING

Zoom gives you the privilege to record calls as videos. This requires permission, as it depends on the host to enable recordings in settings.

It is advisable to check if the recording is enabled in your account settings before you get started.

To do that, you have to log into your Zoom account, click on **View Account Settings/Meeting Settings.**

Then, move to the Recording tab; then click **Enable video recording**.

Hosts can activate the Recording option for all participants.

Note: to record a Zoom meeting, you have to choose between local or cloud options to use.

In the **Local** option, you store the Recording manually on your computer or in any other storage area.

In the **Cloud** option, you are required to pay a subscription fee. The difference here is that Zoom automatically stores the video file for you in its cloud storage.

During the course of the meeting, you will be able to see participants that are recording the meeting. At the end of the call, Zoom automatically converts the recording into an MP4 file.

Recording Zoom meetings on mobile phones is possible. This is done by cloud recording which is made available through a paid subscription. To record a meeting:

Open your Zoom app.

Click on **Start a meeting.**

Click the three-dotted menu located at the bottom-right of the screen.

Then, click on **Record**.

Your recording starts. You can also pause the recording whenever you want.

When the Zoom meeting or call is over, you will see your recorded video in **My Recordings**.

Recording transcripts

You can transcribe the audio of any recorded meeting, edit the transcript, scan the transcript text for main keywords to access the video at that moment, and also share the recording.

To transcribe recordings, you have to enable the Audio Transcript feature. To do this, you have to sign into

Zoom using a web browser, and locate **My Meeting Settings.**

After this, you then move to the Cloud Recording tab and ensure it is enabled. Then you turn it on.

CHAT OPTIONS

Access the **Chat** option at the bottom of the main window. It will open a popup window. This will allow you to write comments and send messages during the meeting. You can also upload files or photos from your device, Google Drive, or Dropbox by clicking on the file icon.

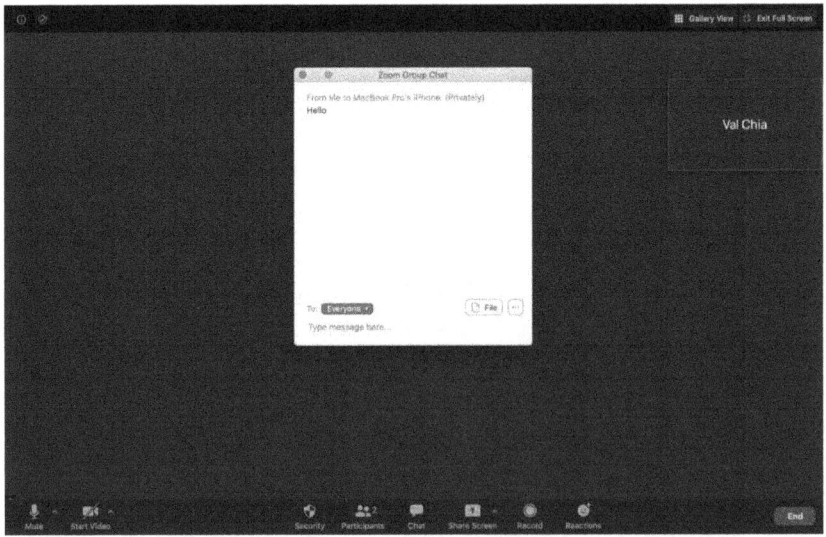

This is particularly convenient if you want to discuss certain specifications during the meeting, such as presentations, reports, or diagrams. In case you wish to send a private message to a participant you will need to click on **Everyone** and select from the list the person that you wish to contact.

RECORD A MEETING

To record the meeting, select **Record** at the bottom of the main window. As soon as you click the option, you will notice a red pulsing icon in the top-left corner of the window. This signal shows that the meeting is being recorded. The participants will also be aware of the recording as the red icon will be displayed beside your name in the vertical window on the right side of the screen. You can also stop or pause the recording by clicking on the respective buttons beside the recording icon.

To access the recording and choose a particular location to save the recorded data, select **Zoom.us** in the top panel of your window and go to **Preferences**.

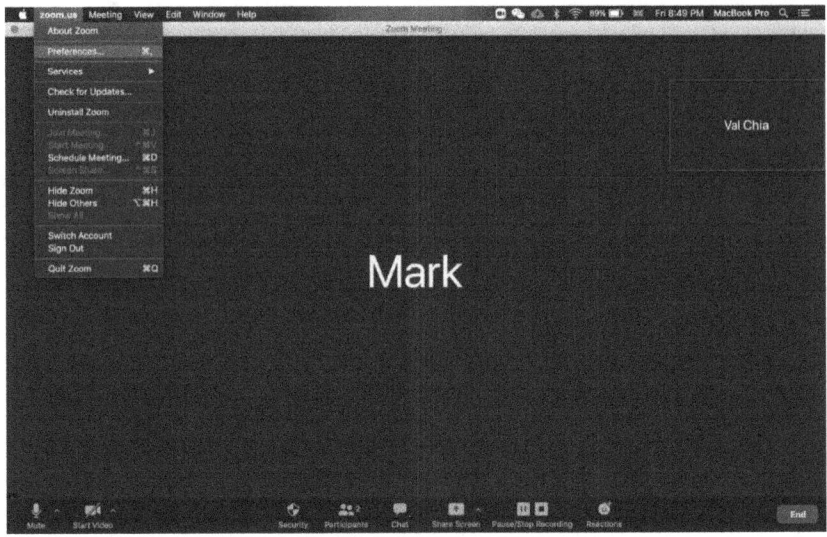

Next, select **Recording** in the left panel. Click on the list beside **Store my recordings at**. Select **Choose a new location**; then select the folder or location that will collect all the recordings.

CHAPTER 3:
ZOOM PRACTICE (ADVANCED)

ZOOM VIRTUAL BACKGROUND

If you just want to do some deep things or you don't want others in the Zoom Call to see the devastating mess in your home, the good news is that Zoom offers a virtual grid. These are support calls that include views of the state, city, and also views of the sea.

VIRTUAL BACKGROUND OPTION

If you have a green room background that contrasts with you, Zoom can do a virtual background. This is something that looks exceptionally good and avoids having to reveal the background of your room, providing us with the option to choose between diverse landscapes, or even upload a photo or video of our own.

To activate this option, we log into our Zoom profile as we have seen before, by going to *https://Zoom.us/signin* and logging in with our Google account.

Once logged in, go to **Settings** and search for **Virtual background**. Turn it on.

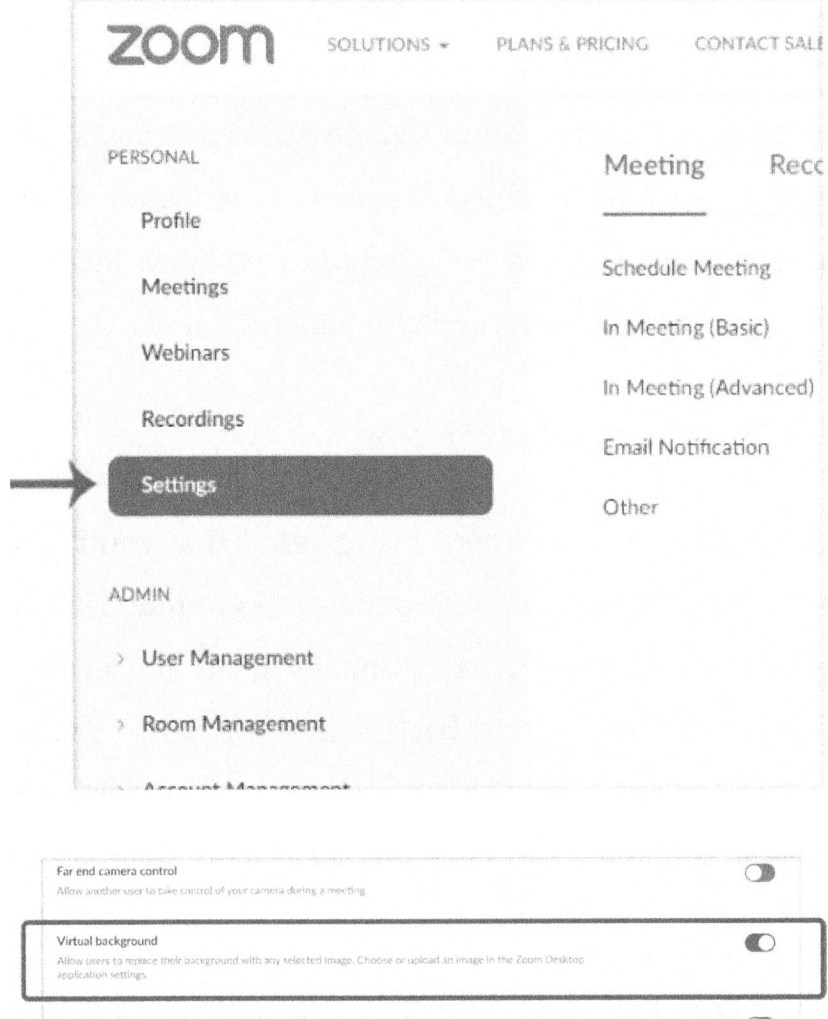

Now, we try finding an evenly green sheet. It doesn't have to be exactly green, but the results are optimized for this color. Try doing it with the colors you have available. There must be no objects so that the background you choose contrasts with our green.

Make sure the light is not overly bright or dark.

To access the virtual background, go to the **Configuration** > **Virtual background** > **Choose the virtual background** (_Note: By clicking on (+), you can upload your background or video_). Click on **I have a green screen** and exit.

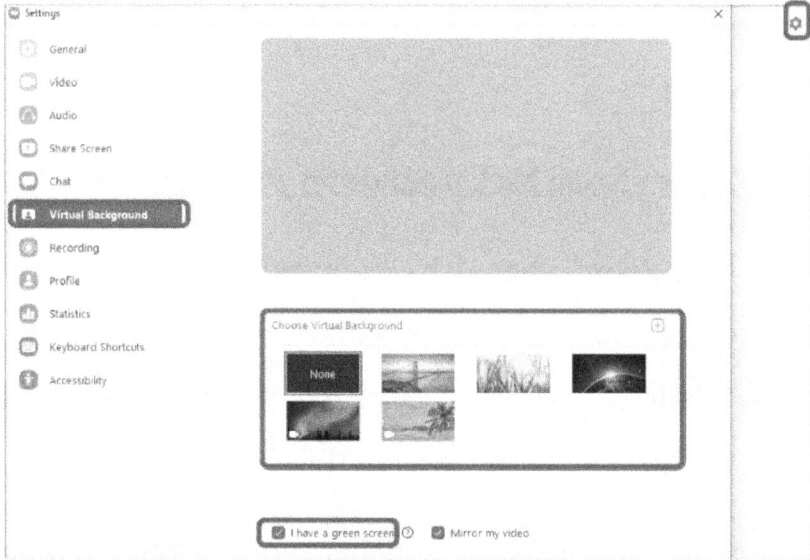

It may seem that we are on the beach or in the mountains, and the result will be like this:

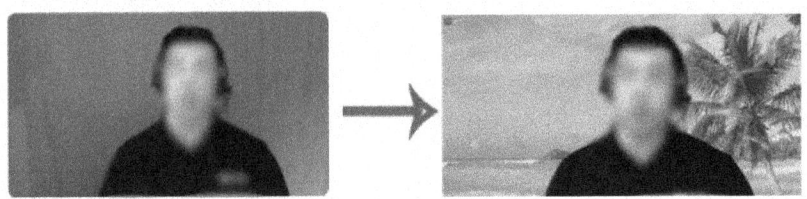

If you want to vary the background during a meeting, go to **Video** > **Video settings**.

Best Zoom Background: Entertaining Virtual Backgrounds for Zoom Meetings

With a virtual background, you can customize your background. It is available for both iPhone and desktop computers.

How to use virtual backgrounds on your desktop

Note that Zoom virtual background feature is fairly easy to use. For example, on a Mac or PC, just open the Zoom client, click on the **Install** icon in the corner, and select **Virtual Background** from the sidebar.

Zoom provides some real backgrounds. Click the one you want to use. Getting your wallpaper, click the plus sign at the apex, and to the left of the background preview, pick an image from your computer and add it. A virtual background can be included while in a meeting. In the Zoom client, press the arrow next to the video icon to the left, click **Select Virtual Frame** and you will see the same virtual page.

The company recommends using a green screen and a good webcam for the best results, but it is possible to use a virtual grid without a green screen.

How to use virtual backgrounds in mobile apps

You can also use virtual backgrounds from Zoom in the app.

Log in to your account and join the conference call. Then, click on the three boxes at the bottom of the screen and click the **Add** menu. Then click on **Virtual background** and select the background to use.

Edit background appearance

In addition to the virtual foundation, Zoom also offers the opportunity to enhance your look during a call. There is an operation called "Touch Your Looks" which is useful if you have not received a daily caffeine fix or are struggling with life in your office.

Touchup your looks with the filter to optimize fine lines. It is designed to look very natural. To use it, go to **Settings** and select the touchscreen for touching on the Video tab.

How to Record Straight to iCloud

In addition to recording Zoom meetings, you can also automatically copy the audio of the meeting you are recording to the cloud. As meeting guests, you can edit the text, scan the text of your keywords to make the video happen at that moment, and share the recording.

To permit the audio file operation for your use, visit the Zoom portal and proceed to **Meeting Settings**, then **Cloud Storage** on the Recording tab, and affirm that the setting is allowed. Click **Apply** if not so. Once the option is gray, it will be under the key sign at either group or account levels and you must call your Zoom Manager.

Zoom Gallery

Viewing the presentation, 49 participants in the meeting can be seen, not the default 25, although it depends on the device.

The Zoom software on Android and iOS permits you to start or join a meeting. As it comes, the Zoom application screen is visible over the active speaker. When more participants are entering the meeting, you will see a thumbnail of a video in the lower right corner. You can watch videos from up to four participants at a time.

Zoom allows MacOS or Windows to view 49 people. When the desktop application is installed on your computer, go to **Settings** and click **Video** to display the Video Settings page. Then proceed with the option **Showcase up to 49 participants in a box view**.

Sharing the Zoom screen and pause sharing

Did you know that you can not only share the screen (smartphone and desktop) but pause the screen? Just press the pause button when you do not want the attendees watching you shuffle the presentation slides. Learn more here.

Share and comment on your mobile phone

You can share files directly from your phone while you are in a meeting and use your phone's tablet function by typing notes with your finger. To make notes while viewing someone else's danger screen, click **Show Settings** at the top of the Zoom window, and then click **Notes**. A toolbar appears with all the options of markup such as text, drawing, arrow, and so on.

Zoom in on shortcuts

At telephoto meetings, you can use a variety of shortcuts to access features or change settings easily. They include many, but following are some:

Alt + A + Shift + A: Mute/Unmute

Alt + M + Control + M: Mute/Disable everything except the hosting provider

Alt + S + Control + S: Get started on screen sharing

Alt + R + Shift + R: Start/Stop recording locally

Alt + C + Shift + C: Start/Stop cloud recording

Alt + P + Shift + P: Pause or resume recording

Alt + F1 + Shift + W: Switch to the live speaker on video conferencing

SECURITY AND PRIVACY AT ZOOM

There have been a lot of talks lately about Zoom security. To tell the truth, it has been questioned, especially since it was made known to the general public as a result of the confinement.

Remember what happened with Houseparty. The smartphone app suffered a massive loss of users when the rumor spread that it contained malicious code that stole your access data to other applications, such as Netflix or your bank accounts

The known issues Zoom has had are discussed below.

Zoom-bombing

- People who access the meeting to torpedo it.
- Facebook collected user data when connecting to Live.
- Theft of data through the Windows application.

The first is something that can happen in any application. Someone gets the link to the meeting and steps in with no other intention than to disturb. We will see how to prevent it, but you can always kick him out of the meeting and it's over.

The second was due to a vulnerability in the code that connected Zoom with Facebook through which the famous social network obtained personal data such as the IP of viewers. They fixed the security flaw with the new update.

The third is solved. In Spain, there was a case of Zoom installation and two days later they suffered a bank fraud of €19,000. The Civil Guard investigations have concluded that these events are not related to each other.

It is true that there was a security flaw (solved with the update to the new version) that allowed access to Windows documents but, in no case, to the bank account.

Everything else are rumors and commercial interests that have been enhanced by the radical ban on Zoom by some famous companies.

One of the upsides to Zoom having these cyberattacks is that it has greatly enhanced its security. Cybercriminals have inadvertently contributed to increasing the list of benefits of this software.

Key settings for keeping harmony in classrooms

Despite the fact that you can utilize a similar meeting ID for each class, Zoom suggests that instructors utilize different meeting IDs/passwords.

Meeting password

When a member physically enters a gathering ID, they are prompted to enter the secret password.

Mute

Members can (and should) mute themselves when they're not talking. Teachers can likewise mute participants individually or at the same time and can set up the gathering to naturally mute all members after entering.

Chat

The instructor can control whether meeting participants can chat openly and secretly during a gathering.

Disable video

As a member, you can get the gathering together with sound just and afterward turn on the video once you're prepared. Instructors can likewise incapacitate an individual member's video.

Virtual feedback

These discretionary little symbols let Zoom meeting participant lift their hands, offer a go-ahead or disapproval, all without intruding on the class.

Lock the meeting

Instructors can lock a Zoom meeting so nobody else can enter until the host/teacher permits it.

Waiting room

Participants are held in a virtual room, and the instructor accepts them individually to ensure no stranger gets access.

File transfer

Images, GIFs can be transferred through the chats except if the host disables this component.

Zoom backgrounds and Noise

The background of some teachers and participants in a Zoom meeting could be a source of distraction, especially for teachers. Teachers can prefer to share their presentation slides. The host can block the videos and mute the audio of participants.

TIPS FOR USING ZOOM SAFELY

Having clarified the problems that Zoom has had, let's see how you can prevent future problems so that your security is not affected.

While it is true that there is no manual to make a meeting by Zoom 100% safe, it is true that you can take a series of precautionary measures so that it does not happen.

The first three are essential. The rest are recommended, although you can lose features or slow access to the meeting.

Update to the latest version

Whether you are using the application for Windows, iOS, or Android, it is essential that you have the latest version installed. Zoom will remind you every time you walk in and haven't done the last update.

Install an antivirus

Whatever your operating system, you should have a paid antivirus, if possible. You pay hundreds of euros to buy it and zero to protect it. The content is more important than the device itself.

Add a meeting password

When you create a meeting, Zoom generates a new default ID and adds a password. Both measures are very good to protect you from intruders.

Enable a waiting room

This way, you can filter access. The host has to allow or deny each participant's access. If it is a mass meeting, this option will not be feasible.

Make registration compulsory

Everyone who attends the meeting will have to enter their name and email. In addition, there will be a record of the time you have arrived. Very useful also for roll call.

Avoid using your personal meeting room

It is your room and is associated with your identity within Zoom (ID), so it never changes. This makes it more vulnerable since if someone finds out, they can enter whenever they want. If you have not started a meeting, there is no problem, but if you just entered when you are in a sales session, it can seriously harm you. Zoom had noticed this, and now it is mandatory to establish a password for access to your personal room.

Turn off file transfer

This option is available in the paid versions. Allows you to transfer files between participants. If you are going to use it, do not deactivate it. You can also share files by uploading them to a cloud service (Dropbox, Google Drive, etc.) and pasting the link.

There are additional steps you can take once you have started a meeting. They are found in the bottom bar, on the Security tab.

Lock the Meeting

Restrict access to new participants.

Enable waiting room

As mentioned, each participant requires that you allow them to access the meeting.

Screen Sharing

Activate or deactivate this option for participants.

Attendees' name change

This can be set so that you can identify those present easily.

Chat

You can disable the chat entirely to be attended to.

As you can see, there are many steps you can take to make your meeting a safe place. The essentials are to update to the latest version, install an antivirus, and set a password to enter the meeting.

OPTIONS BAR DURING A MEETING

As a meeting manager, the bar looks like this:

From left to right, we can see:

Mute

To activate/deactivate your audio.

Start video

Activate/deactivate your video.

Security

Allow participants options such as screen sharing, chatting, renaming, etc.

Manage Participants

Members of the current meeting.

Chat

To chat during the meeting. This is effective for people who won't be able to connect the audio or video because they do not have a microphone, webcam, or encounter technical problems in this regard.

Screen sharing

This option allows you to share what you see on your screen with others: presentations, videos, photos, etc.

In the *basic* menu, you can share any window you have opened, such as photos, presentations, videos etc. This option is the most used in most cases.

In the *advanced* menu, you will be able to share only a part of the screen of your choice, in addition to being able to share the audio generated by your computer without the video.

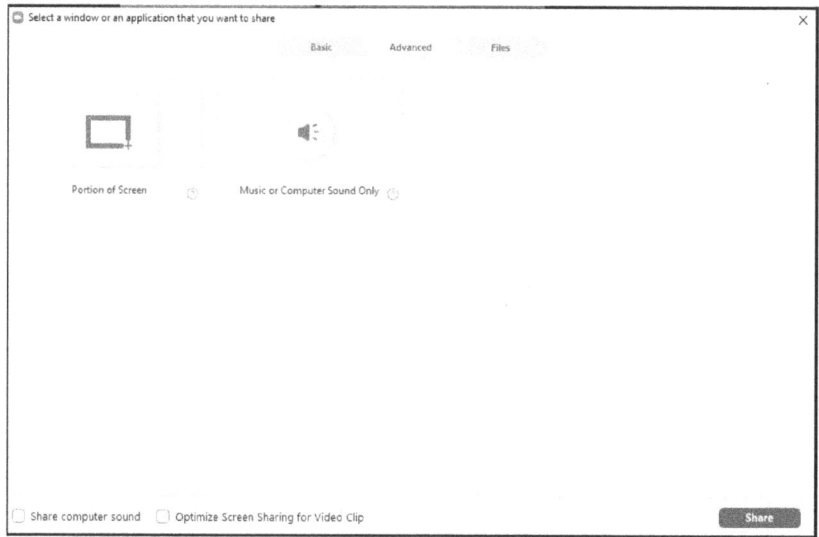

In the **Files** menu you can send a file such as a PDF, PPT, MP3 or MP4 file.

To finish sharing, just click on **Stop Sharing**.

WHITEBOARD OPTION

In **Screen Sharing** > **Basic Menu**, we can find the whiteboard option.

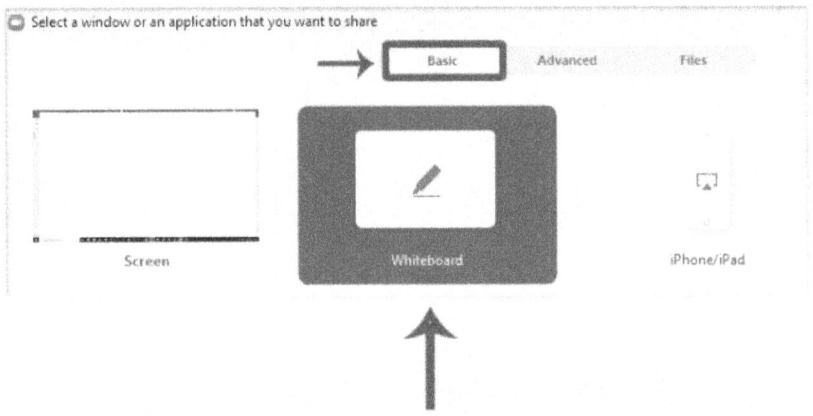

Here, we can share a virtual whiteboard, ideal for any type of class that requires notes and explanations.

The interface is shown below:

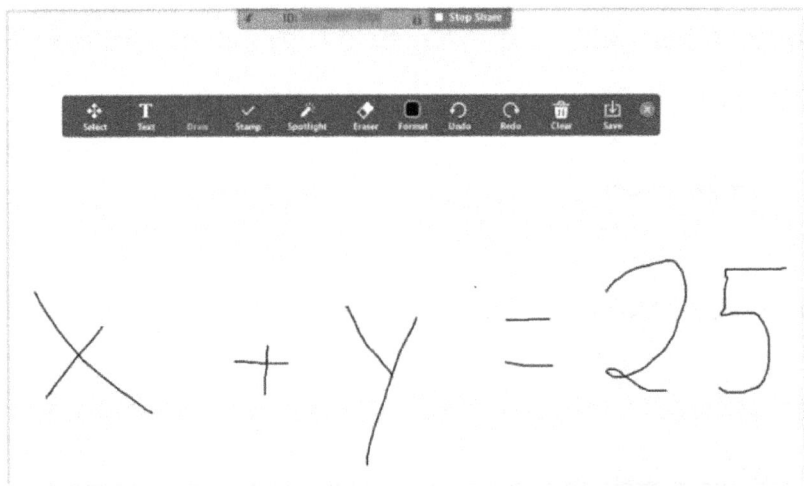

We have an option bar to select, include text, draw, erase, color, etc.

We additionally have the option **Save** to save our photo from the board on our computer.

Let's continue with the options on our main bar:

Record

Record the current meeting to make it available for later. You can store the file in MP4 at the end of the meeting.

When we are done, we will click on the **End meeting** and our file will be saved on our computer. By default, the destination folder will be opened. If not, it will be saved to *C:\Users\(your username)\Documents\Zoom.*

They can also be accessed via **Configuration > Recording > Open.**

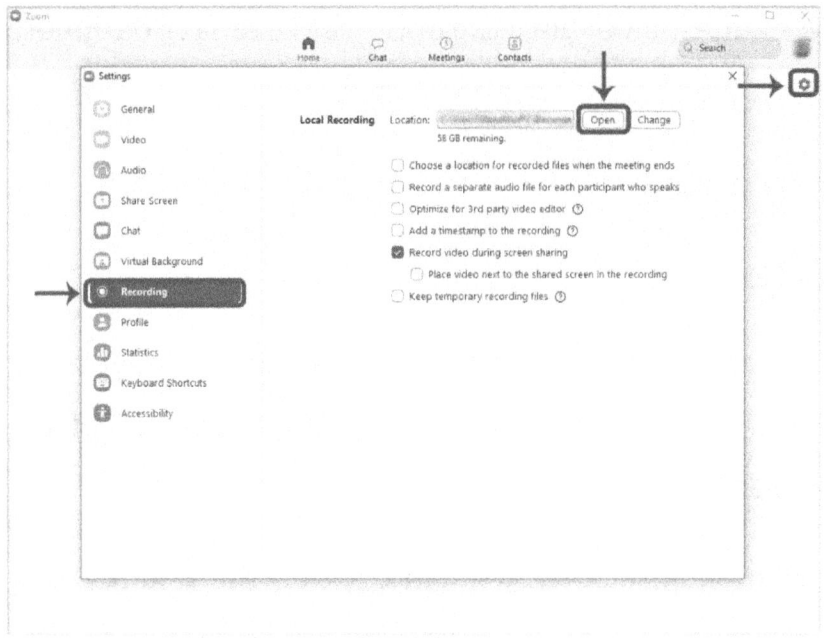

Reactions

Introduce emoticons to encourage the interlocutors.

As a participant, the options bar is practically the same. In this case, the **Security** function is unavailable.

REMOTE CONTROL

During a meeting, you can request for remote control of someone's computer. This option is immensely useful when you are explaining something to someone else, and they are unable to do it successfully. We can take over their mouse and keyboard remotely to execute actions on their computer.

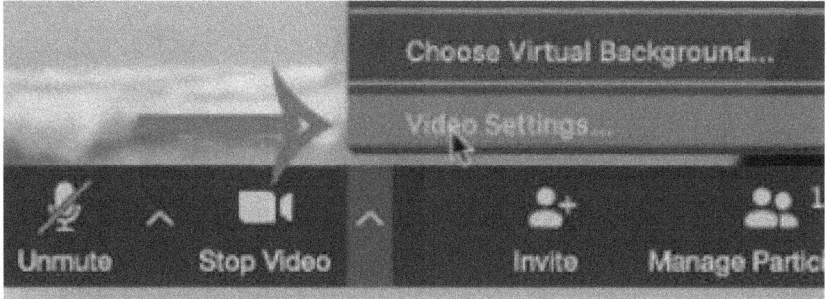

To activate it, the person from whom we want to remotely control the computer must share their screen by using the **Share screen** option.

Once this is executed, you should go to the menu at the top of the screen and click on **View options > Request Remote Control**.

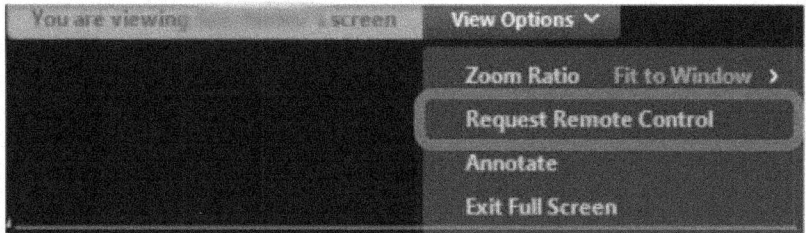

The other person must ACCEPT to start the remote control and we can now control their computer.

To finish, go back to the **View Options** menu and stop the remote control.

KEYBOARD SHORTCUTS

In the **Configuration** > **Keyboard shortcuts** menu, we can find the shortcuts to receive a more efficient experience, so by pressing the key combinations we can execute certain functions and save time.

Take a look to see which one best suit your meeting features.

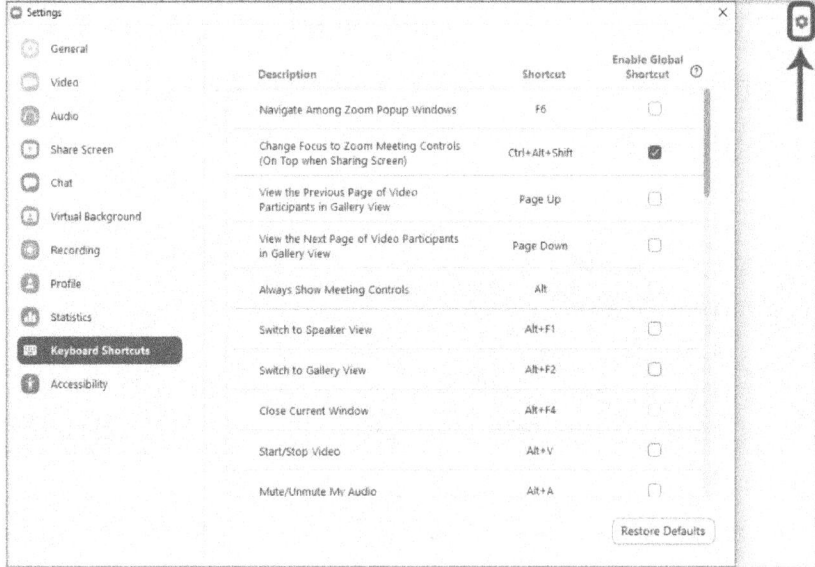

MEETING CONTROL

Meetings and web control are similar, with only a few different options.

Figure 14: Zoom Meeting Panel

Here you can get all the necessary options to personalize, including audio and video settings. You can use the audio button to quickly stop your flow. You can also use it to change the microphone and change it for your output speakers.

If your signal is not ideal and you prefer to change it dial audio, press leaves computer audio.

Clicking on the audio option will take you to the main settings screen. There is also an opportunity to check your audio and video files if necessary, audio and video sections are required here. See the options section for more details. Similarly, the video button can be used to stop or change the video source and access to the main settings panel as audio settings.

Figure 15: Zoom Audio Settings

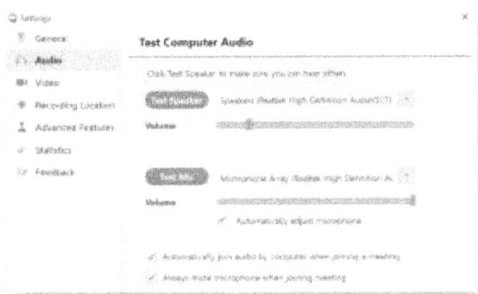

Figure 16: Zoom Video Options

PARTICIPANTS' INVITATION

You can be invited to an open meeting at any time that the participants joined. You can invite them by email, or through the contact list. You can also copy the meeting URL or copy the invitation to the meeting using the lower-left buttons.

Also, give the person who is calling the meeting ID, which is shown at the top of the invitation panel. The sample photos are for meeting number 309-411-140. If you start the meeting in your meeting room, there will be another meeting number.

Figure 18: Control of participants – Al

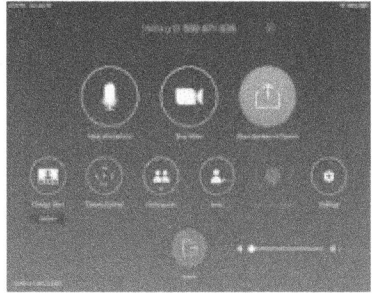

SHARING SCREENS (PART TWO)

In Zoom meetings, you have the opportunity to share your screen. You can choose to share your desktop or specific program either the window you opened. If you choose a particular app and are going to navigate outside of that app when sharing, this will be the source pause until you return to this app.

If you decide to share a video on your computer, be sure to check the sharing computer audio box that provides audio shares a video group. You want to keep all participants silent until you have shared the video promptly.

Extended sharing options

There are advanced sharing options for meetings. This includes allowing one or more participants to participate once again. Just limit or share with the host when participants can share their screens.

Figure 25: Advanced Sharing Options

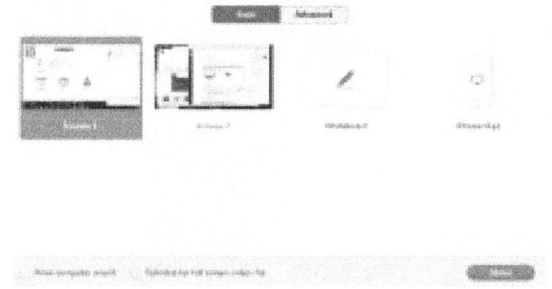

CHAT SETTING

The chat button allows you to open a group chat a meeting. This will be displayed to the right of the video files. You can talk to everyone and only the host. You can use more buttons to limit the possibility of meeting attendees talk to everyone and only the host.

You can also turn off chat for meetings on the web browser Zoom page. For meetings, the chat is a good way to send participants with questions or communication difficulties, especially if they exited audio or video files do not stand out from the crowd.

Figure 26: Zoom Chat Meeting

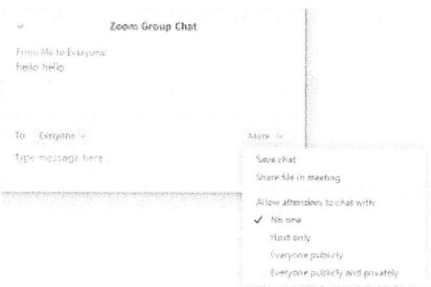

Record

Use the **Record** button to record the meeting. Records are stored on your local computer. Be sure to let all participants know that the meeting has been recorded.

Zoom Tips and Tricks

Require Self-Identification

When making use of Zoom, it is sometimes impossible to meeting members to see the person who is hosting the meeting. It is important to see the person who is talking, but the body language of the person may provide more clues into understanding the subject matter. Imagine a scenario in which meeting members introduce themselves by saying their names before proceeding to share a thought or asking a question. Until people in a meeting become familiar with the person heading a meeting, there is a certain level of communication that may not be achieved.

Make Proper Use of the Microphone

This step is a very important step because it ensures that everyone participating in a Zoom meeting or lecture is carried along. People participating in a meeting may also have to make use of the Chat function to pass a request to the person chairing a meeting to get them unmuted so that they can pass information to the other participants. Most video conferencing rooms have a provision for a microphone. A microphone ensures that all sounds from one part of the conferencing room (that is directly in contact with the microphone0 are heard in other parts of the room. These include side commenting, whispering, sneezing, eating, page-turning tapping, pencil, a sound made while eating, etc.

Set a Standard of Protocol

When setting a standard protocol for a Zoom meeting, some of these points will help you make the meeting more effective:

- Do not indulge in shuffling paper, side communication, noise-making, and pen-tapping. When this is done, the microphone can easily pick it, which will be a major distraction to other participants. For these reasons, it is a best practice to turn off the microphone function. Any member who has something important to say can indicate in the chat feature so that they can be unmuted to speak.

- To avoid causing distractions to others, it is also in your best interest not to engage in activities like drinking, eating, and chewing gum.
- Strive to make eye contact with the person chairing a meeting when he/she is talking by focusing on the position where the camera is, as this will help you in positioning yourself better to learn more.
- To encourage the instructor, it may be nice to nod your head and pay close attention to the information that he/she is passing on.
- When you want to ask a participant a question, directly state their name to have them give you their attention. To this end, it is important to get yourself familiarized with the participants before the start of the meeting.

Participating in a Meeting on Camera

Have the following points at the back of your mind when you are participating in a Zoom meeting or video conference on camera:

- Make sure that you are already set for the lecture or meeting a few minutes before the start of the meeting. If you are the chairperson of the meeting, this is a particularly important step as it helps you test the video and audio connections to ascertain if they are functional.
- Mute your microphone when you are not speaking to students at remote sites. Also, have students at all sites mute their microphones when they are not speaking to avoid feedback.
- When you are not directly speaking to any participant in the meeting, it is a wise decision to have your microphone muted. This step will help you contain any disturbance on your part.

If you are the instructor, maintain eye contact with the rest of the participants at different locations. Make sure that you create unnecessary attention for someone by selecting staring at only him/her. If possible, let your gaze be random but let it carry the same effect as when you will talk to just one person.

Also, when speaking, speak as though you are in a conventional face-to-face meeting or lecture. Close doors and windows, turn off your cell phones, and turn off the noise that emanates from your computer to keep off unnecessary sounds.

- During the process of delivering a presentation, sharing videos, files, or images, do not forget to give the grace of 2-3 seconds or a delay in transmission. You can also do this with audios too. When you are done making a comment, pause to give the other meeting members the opportunity to assimilate and respond to the message, prior to continuing to the next visual or discussion.

- Make it a routine to check the level of coherence of the participants of the meeting to see if they can hear and understand what you are communicating.

Collaboration and Pedagogy Ideas

When you are preparing for a Zoom meeting, let these ideas be your ideals.

- *Make sure that you have a clear idea of what you want to share.* You may also like to consider availing an agenda or plan for each meeting to the participants to make the meeting a smooth and comprehensive one. When this is done, it is almost always a certainty that the object of the meeting will be achieved. Each plan/class agenda can reiterate the desired etiquette.
- *Discuss your plan and agenda.* Keep yourself within the intended series of events, and have it at the back of your mind to keep the participants of the meeting engaged.
- *Have question and answer sessions.* As explained before, reserve some time for the explanation of some concepts or discussion of certain topics for the benefit of your class of participants. When you put this into, give the participants the benefit of time to dish out their response. Most times, it may take time, and also, network connectivity may interfere with how fast you get to hear them when they eventually speak. Participants ought to provide their feedback to their instructors to them both

parties on the same page and help them not to be lost in the midst of a sound video conference

- *Break-out groups.* Before significant group conversation, consider offering a small amount of class time for a group activity or using the "think-pair-share" technique to have participants.
- Let participants make use of annotation tools during conferencing.
- Sometimes, make the participants the presenter to allow them to share their thoughts, projects, ideas and etc. with the rest of the participants.

Concepts for Utilizing Zoom as a Screencasting Tool

- Create annotated and narrated mini-lectures and slide lectures.
- Create introductions and overviews for courses if that is the object of the meeting.
- Create tutorials and screen recordings for web tours, filling out forms, software programs, and etc.

SOME TRICKS FOR UTILIZING ZOOM FOR SCREEN-CASTING

Keep video lessons/segments short

- Use animations, images, and visuals economically when they assist in passing a message.
- Keep text on a slide or page to the lowest when projecting text. When the text becomes too much, or too small so that it doesn't fit onto one page or slide, it will become almost impossible to read through Zoom screen sharing.
- Use the annotation tools of Zoom to point out certain information or bring the students' attention to a major point.
- Create embedded or guided activities or questions for the participants to do when they are done watching a video. But then, this is entirely a function of the intent of the meeting in the first place.

Test knowledge with self-assessment and quizzes.

CHAPTER 4:
ZOOM FOR WORK

How to Teach Online with Zoom

One of Zoom's most interesting possibilities is to teach online. In this way, you can impart your knowledge from your home to the rest of the world. And yes, I say to the rest of the world. Your students only need an Internet connection and a device to connect to.

Today, we all carry a smartphone in our pockets, so no problem.

Lately, I have received many emails from teachers (from academies, colleges, universities) asking me if Zoom was useful to continue teaching. The answer is "*yes.*"

It is also useful to take exams. Perhaps it would be wiser to take an oral exam or take a test-type exam with limited time. This would reduce the chances of the copies, although we already know that they have a special ability. Among all the Zoom versions, we are going to see which ones are worth teaching.

VERSIONS TO TEACH VIRTUAL CLASSES

There are three versions that serve to provide training, whether regulated or not (virtual courses).

Zoom Meetings:

This is the standard version of Zoom. Allows interactive group meetings of up to 100 participants. There are add-ons to reach up to 1,000 simultaneous participants.

Zoom Webinars:

This version turns the platform into a video conferencing tool with the typical webinar format. That is, there is a presenter or speaker who exposes a topic and only he and his screen are seen (if he shares it).

Zoom for Education:

It is designed for large educational institutions. It allows Zoom to be integrated into the classroom and to hold hybrid meetings (with face-to-face and distance students). Twenty hosts can use it at the same time.

Zoom Meetings is the most popular and the most accessible of them all. From €13.99 per month ($14.99) you have access to multiple options such as having group meetings without a time limit, doing surveys, and sharing your live shows on Facebook and YouTube.

Zoom Webinars is geared for more traditional, one-way training. The teacher explains and the rest attend. It has the possibility of obtaining feedback from students by enabling chat and even allowing a particular student to speak. It also works for typical webinars for sale, but that is not the case at hand.

Zoom for Education is a complete package for an innovative educational entity that wants to combine the advantages of face-to-face and online training in a single solution.

Zoom Functionalities for Teaching Online

We have seen some of the most interesting features of Zoom. Now, I am going to detail in which one a high educational potential lies.

Group classes

Sessions can host as many participants as if you were in the classroom. You see and hear the students. You can see their faces as you explain, so you know if they are following you or are in the Yupi worlds.

Live classes

Giving live sessions is something unmatched. Students are connected and share the virtual classroom with their classmates. Camaraderie and feelings of closeness are generated despite the distance.

Deferred classes

If any student is unable to attend live, they can see the recording of the class. Also, if the teacher can't give the class for whatever reason, you can record it earlier and have it play when the time comes.

Tutoring

A close and direct way to have a tutorial with each of your students. Audiovisual communication lowers barriers and helps to empathize. A much more natural way of communicating than a phone call.

Share presentations

Excellent and demands utility for every self-respecting teacher. What would a virtual class be without its PowerPoint or PDF presentation? You can also share the screen to show a photo or an exercise.

Share videos

The possibility of screen sharing opens up a range of possibilities, among which is the sharing of audiovisual content, such as an interview with an expert in a certain subject, a documentary, or an educational video.

Virtual whiteboard

This functionality allows us to turn our screen into a whiteboard. The advantage is that here there is no chalk to stain you and that erasing the board is a matter of clicking. It is very useful to solve exercises and make explanations with graphic support.

Raise your hand

The student can raise his hand as if it were a face-to-face class. The teacher will receive a rather subtle warning on their screen. In this way, you will know that there is a student who has a question and who it is. You can continue with your explanation or stop to solve it.

Create surveys

A very cool feature to make the lesson more enjoyable and participatory. The trainer can ask questions so that the students answer and validate their knowledge.

Chat

This is a very interesting functionality and a double-edged sword. It is interesting because it increases the interaction between the whole classroom; It is dangerous if private chat is activated since students will be able to write to each other without the teacher knowing it and they will be distracted.

Zoom for Business

Though everyone is embracing the videoconferencing app Zoom, you need to have a few skills to ensure you get as many people into your paid or free class to increase your visibility and sales afterward.

These include:

- A good sales copy that grabs the attention of your audience. It should highlight their pain points and show them how your Zoom class can solve it. Also, the benefits they stand to gain.
- The emails generated can be used to follow up on those who registered for the Zoom class. This is to ensure they do not forget and are constantly reminded about the class.
- -Ensure your class is engaging enough.
- -Intermittently ask for feedback from participants during the live session to ensure they can see and hear you, and that network has not truncated the session.
- You can also save the replay (this is optional).

CONCLUSION

One such technology that has made our professional and personal lives better is video conferencing. It has increased our work efficiency, saved time and money, enhanced productivity, and brought about more convenience. The modern era has made it possible to connect with almost anyone in the world through this virtual platform.

If you are planning to start a business as soon as the economy becomes more stable, consider video conferencing services such as Zoom a crucial part of your working conditions. It will not only save you money but also improve productivity, eventually resulting in a decreased turnover and more profits. If you are already running a business, try to incorporate video calls as a part of your regime. And, if you are a current employee of a company, you can suggest this solution to your boss.

When it comes to your family and friends, Zoom is a great way to get everyone together at the same time.

You can host a meeting and chat over a glass of wine, organize a game for everyone to play, or create a quiz. The possibilities are endless.

The Zoom app remains a great tool in maintaining social distancing during this lockdown period.

Even after the pandemic is over, it may still be fully used as it saves energy and time, and causes less stress.

Setting up a Zoom Meeting is as easy as clicking on an invitation connection to start the app or asking users to install the GUI.

It is one good video conferencing software despite a few hiccups with Zoom. Its ability to provide high-definition audio and video quality is outstanding, even though it needs a stronger link to the internet. The benefits overall outweigh the drawbacks, and Zoom is worth it.

Now that you have learned all the features that are available in Zoom, you are trained to use this service with expertise.

While learning the practical aspects of operating a video call and service is important, there are also certain contextual aspects that one must know before leading any virtual meeting. To help you with this, the latter section of this book will teach you ways to be a pro in a video conference along with certain dos and don'ts that will make you an ace in this arena.

To sum it up, Zoom offers excellent support, basic and advanced features that enhance a successful video conference, impressive host and participant controls, thorough engagement, and, now, reliable security, making it a complete package.

Good luck.

CPSIA information can be obtained
at www.ICGtesting.com
Printed in the USA
BVHW080747070521
606655BV00001B/187